CONTENTS

Introduction
HOW FINANCES WORK FOR YOU AND THROUGH YOU FOR THE KINGDOM

W E LIVE IN the richest country in the world in a period of history in which the world as a whole has never seen such a surge in wealth. The world of our grandparents, in terms of their money and assets, was nothing close to what we have today. Regardless of what government definition of poverty you prefer, the poor in America today have more than the middle class did just thirty years ago. In 1970, for example, less than one-third of all families had a car or dishwasher, and less than half had a clothes dryer.[1] Today, over 60 percent of families have two cars, 80 percent have dryers, and over half have dishwashers.[2]

Our magazines, television shows, and advertisements all celebrate wealth, and any bookstore or library is full of titles on how to get rich, how to hang on to your money, or how to "beat the system." With all this interest in money, you'd think someone might stop and ask, What does God say about money? What is God's approach to wealth and prosperity? How should we, as Christians, view money, acquire money, and, above all, use money for His purposes?

More than ever, the body of Christ needs money to spread the gospel. Even the simplest Bible tracts cost money; but getting the attention of people in the twenty-first century—including those in so-called Third World countries—demands much more than simple tracts. Today's distractions (and, in many places, troubles and suffering) are such that sophisticated, yet personal, methods of spreading the good news of Jesus Christ are more necessary than ever. Television costs money. Satellite communication costs money. E-mail programs and Web sites cost money. Airplanes that can carry you to the uttermost parts of the earth cost money.

God knew this from the beginning. He knew that Christians would need money in this age to compete with the secular media. He has always used the technology that was available to spread the gospel—in Roman times, it was the road system; and in the 1500s, it was the printing press. God knows what things cost. He's never surprised by the cost of a gallon of gas or quart of milk.

He knows *we* need money to survive. God understands that Christians, in their daily lives, need to live in a world where costs keep going up. Do you think it would be more expensive or less expensive than it was ten years ago for you to drive across your state to speak to a youth group about Jesus? Of course it's more expensive than ten years ago, and in 1990, it was more expensive than in 1960, and so on. The point is, Christians, who live in this world alongside non-believers, have to eat, buy clothes, and pay for housing. The Bible says God "sends rain on the just and on the unjust" (Matt. 5:45). He doesn't make one gas station only for Christians, with lower prices, and another for non-believers, with higher prices. We have the same normal human needs, which Jesus said our Father knows we face. (See Matthew 6:25–34.)

It's silly, then, to think that God would provide a system for everything else in our Christian life—prayer, marriage, confession of sin, baptism, interpersonal relationships, the government—and not provide a system for dealing with prosperity. And, indeed, He has.

As you will see, there are many misconceptions about wealth. Some of these misconceptions stem from pure ignorance of the Word. Certainly the devil plays a role in keeping Christians ignorant, helpless, and defeated. In our world today, what better tactic could he have than to ensure that most Christians always stayed poor? From the devil's perspective, when you see a wealthy Christian, you see someone who is a tremendous threat to his agenda. That is a person who can leverage money for the kingdom in ways that poor Christians cannot. We have no trouble understanding this in the natural: when charities, political parties, or social causes need to raise money, they hold auctions and benefits. Who attends those? The poor? Not the last time I looked! It's always the rich who are approached for their money. They can leverage money because they *have* it. The church needs to apply this same common-sense approach.

But God's system is vastly different from the world system directed by the devil. An understanding of and an appreciation for God's plan requires a thorough study. You can't yank individual verses out of context as "proof" texts any more than you can for salvation. Unfortunately, the extent that most people know of God's financial plan for His people can be encapsulated in the account of the rich young ruler—a real event and not a parable, and one which is consistently misinterpreted. If you ask the average Christian—one who doesn't study the Word rigorously—what the account of Jesus' interaction with the "rich young ruler" means, he or she will probably say that it tells us that money is evil. In fact, most people will wrongly connect this event with Paul's statement to Timothy that "the love of money is a root of all kinds of evil" (1 Tim. 6:10), and they will likely even misquote that as "money is the root of all evil."

Thank God He established early the principle that every word shall be established in the mouth of two or three witnesses. (See 2 Corinthians 13:1.) Accordingly, we have many passages that deal with wealth, so we can put what Christ said to the rich young ruler in context. And thank God He gave us a clear outline of how Christians are supposed to obtain wealth and what to do with it when we get it.

In this book, I want to show you God's plan for prosperity. Our heavenly Father intends for all believers to be financially secure. Critics want to dismiss this as "name it and claim it" or "blab it and grab it" hocus-pocus. It's nothing of the sort. What I will be discussing in this book is God's very blueprint for how any Christian should conduct his or her life when it comes to money. Prosperity is the *result* of doing God's Word, not the objective. Yes, "money cometh" because Christians, in fact, seek first the kingdom of God.[3]

I want to show you in this book how this is a natural process—in the good sense of the word *natural*, the way God originally created it. You'll see that it's no different than carbon dioxide resulting from the process of photosynthesis or adrenaline being released when you get excited. Prosperity is part of the original design. Unfortunately, Satan has gotten so many people involved in the world's system of wealth creation and distribution over the period of two thousand years that the very concept of prosperity has become corrupted and the purposes of wealth, forgotten.

We will begin by looking at God Himself. Is He poor? How does He live? Then we will examine one of the first godly men, Abraham. How did he live when he was in covenant with the great I AM? What was his financial situation? Next we will examine the law of tithing that was established early in man's history, even before the Mosaic Law, and the role that it plays in prosperity.

There are certain rules of financial wellbeing in God. Tithing and giving offerings is key, and that operates along with the basic rule of sowing and reaping. What happens if you do not tithe? Why is tithing important for *you*? I think after reading the first few pages of this book, you'll see God has more than enough money and doesn't need your measly check every week. So what role does tithing play for the Christian? What happens when you "rob God"? What happens if you pay your tithe to dead or unproductive churches?

Many people say tithing was under the Old Testament, or the old covenant, and we are under the new covenant so it's not relevant. Is that true? What, exactly, is our new covenant with Christ? What does it entail? It is important for the Christian to understand what we have in Christ, because if God says we have it, then who are you to debate God? Further, if God has given us some talent to get wealth, should we not take advantage of it? In fact, it is a sin to fail to use your talents.

We also need to examine the world system of prosperity. How does the world generate wealth? Why is it important to understand the difference between how God makes people wealthy and how the world deals with "the rich"? Why does there seem to be such a spirit of poverty across the world, despite the fact that some of the poorest people on earth live (and have lived for hundreds of years) on some of the richest lands? What is Satan's poverty trap, and why are we admonished not to trust in uncertain riches?

Finally, we will look at God's system for making His children prosperous. What is the "prosperity pipeline"? How is wealth transferred through faith? Perhaps most important of all, what is the purpose of prosperity, and how is prosperity a partnership—a covenant—with God?

Along the way, I think you'll get a much different look at the One—and the only One—who should be our model in all this, Jesus the Christ. How did He handle money? How did He teach His disciples to handle wealth? Was Jesus poor, as so many ministers have led us to believe?

When we are finished, you will have a new appreciation for real "high finance"—the godly kind.

Part I
GOD AND WEALTH

Chapter 1
IS GOD POOR?

I T SEEMS LIKE a silly question to ask, is God poor? It ranks right up there with, is God weak? To their credit, most Christians would rightly reject the notion that God is poor. The problem is most of them can't tell you why.

Let's begin with the obvious: "In the beginning God created the heavens and the earth" (Gen. 1:1). That means God created all the wealth that is in the earth, way back "in the beginning." He created all the gold, all the silver, all the diamonds—all the things that have constituted material wealth through the ages. As far as I'm aware, humans have yet to come close to digging up all the earth's gold, silver, copper, or finding all the diamonds, emeralds, rubies, and so on. Is it safe to say that even today, for all practical purposes, physical wealth is unlimited, insofar as we cannot see the end of it?

If God created all this wealth, is it bad? What did He say when He finished His work on the sixth day? Genesis 1:31 says, "Then God saw everything that He had made, and indeed it was very good." Remember, this is before Adam's sin, so at that point, all was as God had made it, sin-free, corruption-free, and perfect (without blemish). It would not be incorrect to re-phrase it this way, then: "In the beginning God created gold, silver, and diamonds, and said, 'It is very good.'" All I want you to see is that God created wealth in the original sin-free world and didn't have the slightest problem with it. Wealth, therefore—or the material manifestations of wealth that men throughout the ages have come to agree on—was not evil when it was created. It was very good.

Let's look at this passage in Genesis 1 a little deeper:

> In the beginning God created the heavens and the earth. The earth was without form, and void; and darkness was on the face of the deep. And the Spirit of God was hovering over the face of the waters. Then God said, "Let there be light"; and there was light. And God saw the light, that it was good.
>
> —Genesis 1:1–3

It's safe to assume then that whatever God does is good and that around Him can be nothing that is not good. James 1:17 reaffirms that: "Every good gift and every perfect gift is from above, and comes down from the Father of lights, with whom there is no variation or shadow of turning." So if it's good, it must be from God. Since James uses the phrase "*every* good gift," we automatically know that if something is bad (in which case it wouldn't be much of a gift anyway), it surely isn't from God.

If we move down in the first chapter of Genesis, we come to the part where God made man:

> Then God said, "Let Us make man in Our image, according to Our likeness; let them have dominion over the fish of the sea, over the birds of the air, and over the cattle, over all the earth and over every creeping thing that creeps on the earth." So God created man in His own image; in the image of God He created him; male and female He created them. Then God blessed them, and God said to them, "Be fruitful and multiply; fill the earth and subdue it; have dominion over the

fish of the sea, over the birds of the air, and over every living thing that moves on the earth." And God said, "See, I have given you every herb that yields seed which is on the face of all the earth, and every tree whose fruit yields seed; to you it shall be for food. Also, to every beast of the earth, to every bird of the air, and to everything that creeps on the earth, in which there is life, I have given every green herb for food"; and it was so. Then God saw everything that He had made, and indeed it was very good. So the evening and the morning were the sixth day.

—Genesis 1:26–31

Notice that not only was all this very good, it belonged to *man.* God gave it all to Adam. All of the earthly wealth was transferred into Adam's hands. You could say, without question, he was the richest man on earth. If God wanted Adam to have this, then it must be acceptable for men today to have wealth.

God told David:

Hear, O My people, and I will speak, O Israel, and I will testify against you; I am God, your God! I will not rebuke your for your sacrifices Or your burnt offerings, Which are continually before Me. I will not take a bull from your house, Nor goats out of your folds. For every beast of the forest is Mine, And the cattle on a thousand hills.

—Psalm 50:7–10

So God owns the cattle on a thousand hills. All wealth began as God's wealth, and then it was all given to Adam as executor for all mankind.

GOD'S HOUSE

Keep in mind that the earth was made for man, not for God. God already had a place to live. What does God's "house" look like? We know Jesus said, "In My Father's house are many mansions; if it were not so, I would have told you" (John 14:2). In Revelation 21:2, we get a glimpse of what exists in heaven. John said, "Then I, John, saw the holy city, New Jerusalem, coming down out of heaven from God." What exactly is the New Jerusalem? Well, John tells us in Revelation 21:3, "And I heard a loud voice from heaven saying, 'Behold, the tabernacle of God is with men, and He will dwell with them, and they shall be His people.'" Among other things, the New Jerusalem is the "tabernacle of God…with men." Put another way, this is the church, or the physical location, where God and man will physically meet on a regular basis.

I have to constantly reiterate this point: the earth was made for *man* by God, not *for* God. He obviously can come here anytime He chooses, but earth is *not* His home. It's not His primary residence, His zip code, His "crib," as it were. That is because the earth—even the future, recreated earth—is a physical place, while God is a Spirit. Jesus said in John 4:24, "God is [a] Spirit, and those who worship Him must worship in spirit and truth." I use the New King James Version, which says "God is Spirit," but if you look at the same verse in the *Amplified Bible*, it says, "God is a Spirit (a spiritual Being)." The point is, God is not physical and/or material. While He can make Himself physical or material, He exists in His normal form as a Spirit.

This is important for our analysis because New Jerusalem cannot be for God to live in—it is a meeting place for man and God. Can we agree on that? Then get ready, because the next part will knock your socks off. *If New Jerusalem is not made for God—if it's not "God's house"—then we can assume that whatever He has, or whatever He lives in, is richer, wealthier, and nicer by several orders of magnitude than New Jerusalem.* New Jerusalem is, essentially, a single room in His lavish mansion.

So what is New Jerusalem like? John tells us that, too. He wrote:

> And he [the angel] carried me away in the Spirit to a great and high mountain, and showed me the great city, the holy Jerusalem, descending out of heaven from God, having the glory of God. Her light was like a most precious stone, like a jasper stone, clear as crystal. Also she had a great and high wall with twelve gates, and twelve angels at the gates, and names written on them, which are the names of the twelve tribes of the children of Israel: three gates on the east, three gates on the north, three gates on the south, and three gates on the west. Now the wall of the city had twelve foundations, and on them were the names of the twelve apostles of the Lamb. And he who talked with me had a gold reed to measure the city, its gates, and its wall. The city is laid out as a square; its length is as great as its breadth. And he measured the city with the reed: twelve thousand furlongs. Its length, breadth, and height are equal. Then he measured its wall: one hundred and forty-four cubits, according to the measure of a man, that is, of an angel. The construction of its wall was of jasper; and the city was pure gold, like clear glass. The foundations of the wall of the city were adorned with all kinds of precious stones: the first foundation was jasper, the second sapphire, the third chalcedony, the fourth emerald, the fifth sardonyx, the sixth sardius, the seventh chrysolite, the eighth beryl, the ninth topaz,

the tenth chrysoprase, the eleventh, jacinth, and the twelfth amethyst. The twelve gates were twelve pearls: each individual gate was of one pearl. And the street of the city was pure gold, like transparent glass.

—Revelation 21:10–21

This passage is astounding, and we might not get the whole impact because of the Old English biblical language retained even in the New King James Version. A furlong is 660 feet, so if you adjust the terminology to miles, you see that the above passage describes a city that is *one thousand five hundred miles on each side*, and *one thousand five hundred miles high*. The thickness of the wall, 144 cubits—a cubit is about one and one-half feet—is 72 yards. Each wall had twelve layers or "foundations" 125 miles high, consisting of these twelve jewels. I'm no jeweler. I don't have one of those little glasses you put on to assess the quality of a gem. However, clearly one and one-half miles *each* just of topaz, beryl, jasper, and sapphire would constitute wealth beyond which the richest American or the Sultan of Brunei could even imagine.

We see in verse 18 that the city was of pure gold. Remember, this is a city 1500 miles *square* of pure gold. Then we see that there are twelve gates, and since John does not comment otherwise on it, we must assume that each gate is as tall as the wall it is attached to. Each one of these twelve gates consists of a single giant pearl. (I'd like to see the oysters these pearls came from!) Imagine a pearl 1500 feet tall!

So if we cannot see heaven—if we cannot see where God lives—we can get just a taste of it in what the Lord revealed to John about the New Jerusalem. It's a city of such astounding, fantastic wealth that it boggles the mind of man. God is not poor.

Consider something else. Imagine the richest person you can think of (and the most recent list of worldwide billionaires puts Bill Gates of Microsoft at the top, with $56 billion in personal wealth).[1] Whether the billionaire in question is a Christian or not, the wealth he has acquired originated with God.

Does God Work?

Now I want to ask you a slightly different question: when did God stop working?

Most of you will say, "That's easy. On the seventh day, because that's when God rested." And I'd guess most of you probably think that God hasn't done a thing since that day—but you'd be wrong.

John 5:16–17 records this episode in Jesus' life:

> For this reason [that Jesus had just healed a man on the Sabbath] the Jews persecuted Jesus, and sought to kill Him, because He had done these things on the Sabbath. But Jesus answered them, "My Father has been working until now, and I have been working."

So much for God taking an eternal vacation! Some of you thought He was on a Carnival Cruise Line, just enjoying the blue water off Bermuda! No, our heavenly Father has been working since resting on the seventh day. Look at Isaiah 28:21: "For the LORD will rise up as at Mount Perazim, He will be angry as in the Valley of Gibeon—That He may do His work, His awesome work, And bring to pass His act, His unusual act." This was not the "work of salvation" per se, but a reference to God routing the Philistines through David. Ephesians 1:19–20 says:

> And what is the exceeding greatness of His power toward us who believe, according to the working of His mighty power which He worked in Christ when He raised Him from the dead and seated Him at His right hand in the heavenly places.

Throughout history, God has been working *with man* in completing the fullness of salvation. First, He had to find a man who would keep a covenant, and He worked with Abraham. Then He had to find a king who would be obedient, and He worked with David. Then He had to find a woman who would bear the Son, and He worked with Mary.

Now, in the new covenant, He works with us! Paul wrote in 1 Corinthians 3:9, "For we are God's fellow workers; you are God's field, you are God's building." You are a "fellow worker" with the Lord of the universe! John said of Jesus (1 John 3:8). For six thousand years, at least, God has been working through His faith, calling those things which be not as though they are! (See Romans 4:17.)

God is not poor. He has created all wealth—and not just what we today call wealth, like money, stock portfolios, diamonds—but even the intangible forms of wealth such as intellect, talent, and energy.

In Hebrews 11:1 Paul wrote:

> Now faith is the substance of things hoped for, the evidence of things not seen.

Wealth is also both things we can see and things we cannot see or touch.

THE ECONOMIC PRINCIPLE OF GIVING

God's principle for tapping into those things we cannot see or touch is to give. "Give and it will be given to you: good measure, pressed down, shaken together, and running over" (Luke 6:38). This principle works even if you aren't a Christian. Lot, who did not believe as Abraham believed, nevertheless followed Abraham and was blessed. A bank pays interest to a Buddhist and a Hindu the same as it pays interest to a Christian. It's the same interest rate for all three. The system works for all who use it. God's whole *modus operandi* is to give. John 3:16 tells us, "For God so loved the world that He gave His only begotten Son." God gave to Abraham for his obedience. The business principles they teach in school of saving and investment are forms of sowing and reaping—delaying gratification today for a better return tomorrow. We tend to think of giving only in the sense that someone donates to the Red Cross or a church. However, the investment of one's time, energy, talent, and abilities *without a guarantee of reward* is covered in the law of giving.

Think of Bill Gates, the richest man in the United States. How did he get all that money? He gave. No, he doesn't give away his Microsoft products free, but early in his career he created a computer operating system that made it easy for average people to use a personal computer. How many people do you suppose turn on a computer every day with a Bill Gates-inspired product in it? Billions? And how many times a day does each of those people use one of the programs he created? Dozens. The production of this very book, in many ways, used some Microsoft operating system somewhere. Well, just think if you actually had to deposit a penny or a nickel into some slot every time you use one of his products. You can imagine how he got the fortune that he has today

21

when you consider that these billions of people were actually doing that dozens of times a day through their purchases. Literally in an hour, he would make millions of dollars. But it began with him investing his time, giving his talent and energy to create a computer system. I'm not making any comment on the business practices, good or bad, of Microsoft or any other company; I'm just making a point about how the business system is based first and foremost on giving.

God knew what He was doing when He said, "Give, and it will be given to you" (Luke 6:38). That is a scriptural principle, but this law works in the business world, too.

Since God is not poor, all wealth originates with Him. Again, I'm not just talking about physical wealth. Every idea, every concept, every process conceived by man originates with God. We see this in Deuteronomy 8:18, which says, "And you shall remember the LORD your God, for it is He who gives you the power to get wealth." God "gives you the power" to get all things. Well, how can God give you something He doesn't have? So God must have the "power to get wealth" before man ever had it! If we get wealth today by inventing, coming up with new computer programs, new drugs, new forms of entertainment, then it was God who had those concepts in the spirit realm before we ever got the idea.

Moreover, God cannot give you the power to get something He doesn't already possess. You may pervert an idea into something sinful, but the perversion did not come from God. It came from Satan. More important, God cannot give you the power to "get poor-ness," if you pardon my English. There is no poverty in God! He can't give you what He doesn't have. If you get poverty, it isn't coming from God, because God is *the* originator of all wealth in the universe—all physical wealth, material wealth, and intangible wealth (including talent, ideas, competence, and stamina). By His very nature, God is rich in everything He does.

So how do we tap into the wealth that God has provided for us? Usually some physical action is also needed to transform the idea into a product or process, but it all begins with the intangible, the "evidence of things not seen" (Heb. 11:1). It all begins with faith.

Our God is a faith God. Whatever He does is done through faith. He isn't a lazy God. He has worked since the beginning, working the work of salvation. And now we are co-workers with Him. While spreading the gospel takes physical work—going on missionary journeys, handing out tracts, translating the Bible—above all, it takes faith. It takes faith for someone to start a new church. It takes faith for that family without much income to tithe. It takes faith to spend hours studying the Word without a physical guarantee that you will be better off. That faith, in God's system, becomes substance. It becomes real to us. What is unseen in the spirit world can be made manifest in the physical world through faith, the "evidence" or proof of things "not seen," but which exist nonetheless.

God is not short on faith. In fact, He's the inventor and designer of faith. He holds the very first faith patent ever issued...and He issued it! All wealth originates in faith. Yet the wealth of this world, as vast as it is, is like a grain of sand compared to the wealth that God lives in. God is not poor. Our Daddy, *Abba* Father, is the originator of prosperity.

WAS JESUS POOR?

The first thing people will say when you make this point is, "Well, Dr. Price, you know Jesus was poor. He didn't have any place to lay His head." Then they will cite Matthew 8:20, which quotes Jesus as saying, "Foxes have holes and the birds of the air have nests, but the Son of Man has nowhere to lay His head." That's not at all what this verse means, because Mark 4:38 tells us that Jesus "was in the stern, asleep on a pillow." Now, I know that this does not mean He had a house, but I'm trying to show those of you that are literalists that you must read everything, not just a couple of verses as proof texts. If you look at Matthew 13:1, it says, "On the same day Jesus went *out of the house* and sat by the sea." I doubt that He owned the house—what would be the purpose in Him buying a house that He would have to default on the mortgage in three years?—but obviously He had money to rent.

So it's easy to think that Jesus had no money and was, in every sense of the word, "poor." Paul said in 2 Corinthians 8:9, "For you know the grace of our Lord Jesus Christ, that though He was rich, yet for your sakes He became poor, that you through His poverty might become rich." For centuries, people have interpreted that to mean that Jesus had no material goods and that we should aspire to be like Him in His poverty. However, this is an incorrect understanding of that verse, which refers to His *status* as King in heaven, who took on the lowly form of a man that we might be kings with Him! However, if Jesus did not flaunt His money, I submit to you that He was exactly the perfect model of how to *leverage* money for kingdom purposes. In order to leverage money, you have to have some. So, did Jesus have money?

Matthew refers to the fellows who sought out the young Jesus as the "wise men." Other translations of these *Magi* say they were "kings." Whether each one was *the* king of his region is up for debate, but clearly they were well-off enough that they could all take off work for months, bringing servants and sufficient money with them that they could come from as far as China (one tradition holds that one of the wise men was a representative of the Chinese courts). Nowhere in the Bible is the number three mentioned as a headcount for the Magi. Our modern nativity scenes all have three wise men because someone took the number from the three types of gifts that were offered. But some scholars think that far more than three were present. Merely crossing the Middle East back then was dangerous, subject to raiding hordes of bandits. Typically, a handful of people had no chance of surviving—they had to travel in large, heavily armed caravans. Some scholars have claimed that up to one hundred wise men were present. It's certainly reasonable to assume more than ten, and perhaps twenty, arrived in Judea.

They did not come to the manger. Look at Matthew 2:11: "And when they had come into the house." Not the inn. Not the stable. Joseph's house. They had gone to Nazareth, not Bethlehem. If you put Luke's and Matthew's account of the birth of Jesus together, you'll find that they presented Jesus at the temple in Jerusalem forty days after His birth for a ceremony of sacrifice to the Lord. We don't know if they stayed at the inn in Bethlehem or if Joseph took the family to Jerusalem, but it's pretty clear that as soon as there was room at the inn, there was no more need to stay in the stable. At any rate, Jesus, Mary, and Joseph were in Jerusalem forty days after His birth. Meanwhile, the wise men were searching for Him in Bethlehem, and the star kept leading them on to "where the young Child was" (Matthew 2:9). Then, in Matthew 2:11, it says, "And when they had come into the *house*, the saw the young Child [not the *baby*] with Mary His mother, and fell down and worshiped Him. And when

25

they had opened their treasures, they presented gifts to Him: gold, frankincense, and myrrh" (emphasis added). We don't know that all the wise men gave equal amounts of these. It's entirely possible that gold, being the most useful and convenient of these gifts, would have been brought by the majority of the Magi.

Here we have a scenario in which, at minimum, Joseph and Mary had several boxes of gold coins, which they assumed control over as trustees for their Son. Both of them knew He was anointed, that He was, as we jokingly used to say, "on a mission from God." But it was true! He was on a mission from the Almighty, and while Mary and Joseph did not know exactly what that calling was, they intuitively knew that at some date in the future, Jesus son of Joseph would be Rabbi and that He would have need of that money. What do you suppose they did with all that gold? Do you think they went to the Roman Riviera and gambled? Maybe they went on a cruise? No! Everything we know about Mary and Joseph was that they were faithful and good Jewish parents, and if they were given money for their Son's future, you can be certain that every penny was there when Jesus needed it for His earthly ministry. Most likely, if there were banks or places they could invest in the Nazareth area, they probably made additional interest for Him.

Isn't it interesting that in one of His parables, Jesus told of a lord who gave his servants his money to watch over while he was away, and one man was given five talents; another received two; and the last, one. When the lord returned, the servant who only had the one talent had buried it and the master said, "So you ought to have deposited my money with the bankers, and at my coming I would have received back my own with interest" (Matt. 25:27). It's not too much to assume that Mary and Joseph, who were selected by God for their obedience, would have at least followed this common sense principle.

At the time of His anointing, then, when He went into the water at the Jordan River, Jesus had at least one, but most likely *many* boxes of gold awaiting Him in Nazareth for His many missionary journeys. He also had the money He Himself earned. Traditionally he is referred to as a carpenter, but back then the term included carpentry and masonry. He was an all-purpose general contractor. Remember Jesus worked with His earthly father Joseph for somewhere between fourteen and seventeen years, depending on when He started earning a wage. Joseph was not a fellow who carved little wooden knick-knacks for sale; he was the Judean equivalent of a union-certified carpenter/mason.

You might think Nazareth was a small town and there wasn't much work. Perhaps, but the county seat of the Galilee region was only three miles away, and a Roman garrison was stationed there. Who do you think most of the carpenters and stonemasons in the region worked for? And the Romans, despite their reputations as harsh occupiers, paid well for quality crafted goods—walls, lookout towers, even spear shafts and ballistas. It's almost certain that Joseph (and Son) were under "retainer" to the Roman army in the region to build wooden tables, chairs, and, yes, even weapons when they needed them. Since the Romans paid well, we can assume that Jesus drew a decent paycheck for somewhere around fifteen years.

What do you think He did with His money? Did He buy a fancy chariot? No. Did He live a party lifestyle? Of course not. He knew, as did His earthly parents, that He was here for a single purpose, and He saved His money just as they saved the money given Him from birth. Therefore, I think we can conclude that between the money given Him by the wise men and the money He earned through work, Jesus of Nazareth had a boatload of money when He entered His earthly ministry.

An obvious reason He did *not* have fancy clothes or ride a nice horse was that He had to select twelve assistant pastors to accompany Him for the next several years. As best we can determine, Jesus knew from the moment of His anointing in the Jordan River that He would have to sacrifice Himself about three and one-half years later. So for three and one-half years, Jesus knew He had to support twelve grown men—feed them, clothe them, pay their taxes, pay all transport fees (you couldn't cross many rivers or the Sea of Galilee at certain places without paying a toll), pay all temple taxes and sacrifice fees, and so on. And He had to do this for three and one-half years. That is some chunk of change! Jesus didn't just run down the road one day saying, "Hey, follow me! I'm gonna be a Rabbi!" Later, in Luke 14:28–30, He would ask His own disciples, "For which of you, intending to build a tower, does not sit down first and count the cost, whether he has enough to finish it—lest, after he has laid the foundation, and is not able to finish, all who see it begin to mock him, saying, 'This man began to build and was not able to finish.'" Jesus was speaking as much of Himself there as of them. He had already counted the cost—not just the incredible spiritual cost of taking on the world's sin, but also the material cost of supporting these twelve disciples for several years.

Here is something else to consider if you are still thinking that Jesus was poor. Would it be just for Jesus, the Son of God, to ask us to do something—rather, *require* us to do something—that He Himself didn't do? No. That would be unfair. It would be like a commander ordering his troops on a march while he slinks back into his tent. How, then, could Jesus say to His disciples and us with any justification whatsoever, "Give..." How could He say, "For I was hungry and you gave Me food; I was thirsty and you gave Me drink; I was a stranger and you took Me in; I was naked and you clothed Me; I was sick and you visited Me" (Matt. 25:35–36). You have to have money to feed people, to clothe them, and even to get from your home to a hospital to visit the sick in this day and age when gas is over three dollars a gallon! So how could Jesus *command* us to give to the poor? To help others?

There is only one way He legitimately could have done that and been consistent with who He is: He would have had to have done it Himself! In addition to using the money He had to support the band of disciples, Jesus was a giver. He gave money away all the time, and in no small amounts. Look at John 13:29, where Jesus and the disciples were celebrating the Passover meal known as the Last Supper. After Jesus told Judas to do his dirty deed, Judas left, and the disciples were puzzled as to why he departed so suddenly: "For some thought, because Judas had the money box." Wait right there. Haven't we been told these disciples were a bunch of homeless, broke bums? So why did they have a money box? We'll look at them separately in a moment. The rest of the verse continues, "For some thought, because Judas had the money box, that Jesus had said to him, 'Buy those things we need for the feast,' or that he should *give something to the poor*" (John 13:29, emphasis added).

It was somewhere around ten o'clock to midnight when this occurred, yet the disciples thought Jesus had ordered the treasurer of the group to suddenly leave and "give something to the poor." Why in the world would they even think that, unless Jesus did it all the time.

We see in the story of the anointing at Bethany that Mary Magdalene came to Jesus and broke an alabaster flask of very costly fragrant oil and poured it on His head as He sat at the table. But when the disciples saw this "they were indignant, saying 'Why this waste? For this fragrant oil might have been sold for much and given to the poor'" (Matt. 26:8–9). Mark adds an interesting detail when he says the disciples—and almost certainly, "the disciples" meant Judas was saying this—said, "It might have been sold for more than three hundred denarii and given to the poor" (Mark 14:5).

A denarius was equal to about a day's wage. Of course things change over time, but I just want you to get a sense of how much this was worth back then. Economic historian Larry Schweikart found that at the 2007 average wage of a construction worker (just over twenty dollars per hour), times eight hours for a typical work day, times three hundred days, you could have a total of $48,000 a year.[2] That fragrant oil Mary broke to pour on Jesus was worth, in modern times, $48,000.

Here's the key: even though the disciples complained about (in their view) "wasting" this in a show of affection for Jesus, none of them thought it at all unusual that they would give away $48,000 to the poor! Why? Because Jesus did it all the time. He had to be a giver. How could He train those men to give to others if they never saw Him give away anything? And yes, He gave His life, but only at the end. They needed to see Him giving money—a lot of money—away, all the time, selflessly. That was the only way they would learn to give. That's why the disciples didn't bat an eyelash when Judas got up from the table in the middle of the night, they thought, to "give to the poor."

Somehow people get wrapped up in some pie-in-the-sky notions that Jesus just walked around and never ate, never slept, never paid any taxes, never had to buy sandals, or never had to do any of the things that ordinary men do. Yet He was both the Son of God *and* a man. When He went into a new town or city, He sent "messengers before His face...to prepare for Him" (Luke 9:52). These disciples arranged lodging, and many times it was not just with friends. They had to pay a deposit. Note that twice when Jesus sent the disciples out without Him, He told them not to take any money. In Luke 9:3 He said, "Take nothing for the journey, neither staffs nor bag nor bread nor money; and do not have two tunics apiece." Then, when He sent out the seventy, He said, "Carry neither moneybag, knapsack, nor [extra] sandals; and greet no one along the road" (Luke 10:4). This was a test, not of the disciples, but of those who would hear His message, for Jesus said if the people took them in they were to "remain in the same house, eating and drinking such things as they give, for the laborer is worthy of his wages" (Luke 10:7).

Now, why in the world would you tell someone *not* to take money if he was a homeless bum anyway and didn't have two nickels to rub together? If I tell you, "Don't bring chewing gum inside the FaithDome," it would be clear that it is your habit otherwise to chew gum. Today, with the security issues, the airport people tell you, "Don't carry sharp objects, fingernail clippers, or nail files aboard a plane." They wouldn't have to say that if it wasn't common for people to bring nail clippers on planes, as we used to do all the time. If these men were all without money, common sense indicates Jesus wouldn't have had to say anything to them about money. You don't tell a homeless bum, "Now, friend, I'm going to take you to lunch, but I want you to leave your Armani suit here with your shopping cart!"

Later, in Luke 22:35–36, Jesus said "'When I sent you without money bag, knapsack, and sandals, did you lack anything?' So they said, 'Nothing.' Then He said to them, 'But now, he who has a money bag, let him take it, and likewise a knapsack; and he who has no sword, let him sell his garment and buy one.'" These men apparently all had moneybags, and all had extra clothes—good enough that their garments would buy a sword. If you don't think that's a pretty good piece of clothing, just try to exchange something in your closet for a hunting knife down at the pawnshop!

I think it is reasonable to believe that Jesus and the disciples, whenever they could, saved money by staying with friends and supporters. He was a rabbi, after all, but a revolutionary one. At any rate, until people heard His message, He certainly would not have had too many friends willing to put thirteen men up for several weeks at a time. Jesus was from Galilee, more than sixty miles from Jerusalem. In those days, without television or radio, word traveled slowly. When He and the disciples went to Jerusalem, especially the first time, it would be highly unlikely that He would have had any friends there, as no one had yet heard about Him.

WERE THE DISCIPLES POOR?

Nor were the disciples themselves homeless bums when Jesus met them. Peter, James, John, and Andrew all had fishing businesses. Mark tells us that James and John worked for their father and he had hired servants and Luke said they had boats (plural). Peter had a house (see Luke 4:38), and it must have been a big one because he lived there with his mother-in-law as well as his wife! Actually, in Mark 3:19, it says after Jesus selected the twelve, they went "into a house," and in Mark 3:20 it says that a "multitude came together again, so that they could not so much as eat bread." That's no small house! Some commentators think this was John's house.[3]

Matthew, a tax collector for the Romans, got 10 percent of every dollar (as it were) that crossed his table. Typically a tax collector waited at one of the gates in Jerusalem, stopped every person who came in with a camel, horse, or cart, assessed what was on the animal or in the cart, and they had to pay a tax right there. Then Levi (as Matthew was called) took his cut off the top. Now, imagine today if you are an IRS agent and you got to keep 10 percent of every return that came across your desk! Levi threw a party for Jesus "in his own house," and it must have been a mansion, because "there were a great number of tax collectors and others who sat down with them" (Luke 5:29). John 7:53 says that after one meeting with Jesus, "Everyone went to his own house." Presumably this means the disciples went to their own houses too. So these disciples—most of them grown men (John, perhaps, was a teenager)—all had homes, businesses, and many of them, families. When Peter said, "Lord, we have left all!" he wasn't kidding.

We have already seen that the group had a treasurer. You don't need a treasurer unless you have "treasure" to keep track of. Moreover, Judas, the keeper of the money box, was stealing from the box the entire time, and Jesus knew it. (See John 12:6.) It may seem odd that Jesus put Judas, whom He knew was tempted by money, in charge of the money box when Matthew, the tax collector, had the only practical experience in the group of dealing with large sums of money. Yet it's completely understandable, in that Matthew was not motivated at all by money, but rather, as his gospel shows, by the need to be proven right. The Gospel of Matthew reads as a giant "I-told-you-so!" to the early Jews. But Judas was motivated by money, and the Lord put him in charge of the money box so he could beat his weakness. Judas, like anyone else, had a chance to trust Jesus or trust money, and he put his trust in "uncertain riches."

Of the other disciples, we know little about their finances, but we know quite a bit about the apostle Paul. Remember, Paul said he knew how to be happy poor and how to be happy rich. Sir William Ramsay, the Oxford archaeologist who wrote on many of the early church figures, developed one of the points about Paul that we always seem to miss: his Roman citizenship virtually assured him to be from an aristocratic family and "may be taken as proof that his family was one of distinction and at least moderate wealth."[4] More-over, Acts 21:39 reports that Paul was "a citizen of no mean [i.e., no average] city," Tarsus, which was a way of saying that "in a provincial city [the citizen of Rome] commonly filled the position of high-class citizens."[5] It is possible he was disowned after his conversion, for Paul wrote in Philippians 3:8 that he had given all up for Christ, "For whom I have suffered the loss of all things, and count them as rubbish." Ramsay argues these are indicative of one who at least at one time had wealth, as is Acts 19:31, where Paul was visited by "officials of Asia." These officials would have had no dealings with someone below their social class.

At the same time, Paul had money to pay the expenses of four poor men who purified themselves in the Temple (Acts 21:23–24). Ramsay adds, "Several other facts show clearly that, during the following four years [at Caesarea and then in Rome], Paul had considerable command of money.

Imprisonment and long lawsuits are expensive."[6] On multiple occasions—with Felix, Princess Drusilla, Queen Bernice—Paul had personal interviews that never would have been granted a poor man, and indeed, had He not been charged with crimes, Jesus Himself would not have been accorded such status! Even more telling, Felix hoped to get a bribe from Paul for letting him go, and "a rich Roman official did not look for a small gift."[7] It was typical for prisoners in any kind of minimum-security prison to pay their own expenses. At Caesarea, Paul was under house arrest and maintained two attendants. Other comforts were *permitted* by the guards, almost always through bribes. In Rome, Paul paid for his own lodging, food, and the wages of the soldier who guarded him. Even the appeals process, which Paul had a legal right to in theory as a citizen, was never granted to poor men. So even though during his missionary journeys Paul worked as a tentmaker, when he needed it, he had wealth.

The disciples weren't poor. Paul wasn't poor. Jesus absolutely was not poor—but He did use His capital entirely for kingdom purposes!

And God isn't poor. Do you want some even better news? He has a plan for our prosperity. Oh, and I bet you can guess it involves faith!

Notes

Notes

Chapter 2
GOD'S PLAN FOR PROSPERITY

T HE FIRST THING to understand about God's plan for prosperity is that He has ordained prosperity for His children. He has a purpose for prosperity: to enable His work to be done on earth. To do that, His vessels on this planet—us—need money. He wants us to prosper. In Psalm 1:1–3 we see:

> Blessed is the man Who walks not in the counsel of the ungodly, Nor stands in the path of sinners, Nor sits in the seat of the scornful; But his delight is in the law of the LORD, And in His law he meditates day and night. He shall be like a tree Planted by the rivers of water, That brings forth its fruit in its season, Whose leaf also shall not wither; And whatever he does shall prosper.

From that passage it seems God wants us to prosper. That is why I pay little attention to those who criticize me when it comes to messages about prosperity, because the Word of God says I *should* prosper. John said in 3 John 2:

> Beloved, I pray that you may prosper in all things and be in health, just as your soul prospers.

So it is God's plan that we prosper.

The first thing you must do is to root yourself in the Word of God. The verse in the psalm says, "He shall be like a tree Planted by the rivers of water." God could have said simply,

39

"He shall be like a tree," but by saying, "A tree planted by the rivers of water," it makes clear that the tree can draw nutrients from the ground and water from the rivers and be sustained. It says that this tree "brings forth its fruit in its season," but you have to be planted—in the Scriptures—before you can bring forth fruit.

Many people have dreams of what they would like to achieve in life, and I can say with virtual certainty that everything they dream of costs money. There is a saying, You can't buy happiness. This is certainly true—if you are not saved, no amount of money in the world will purchase eternal life. And yet it's also true that most of those things that make us *un*happy stem from a shortage of money. If you are sick and need medical care, you can get higher quality care if you have more money. If you can't sleep at night because of bills, obviously money would solve those problems. If you want to bless people but have no cash, again money will allow you to give to other people. It is the same with the things of God: no work of God gets done without finances.

We often speak of people giving "service" or giving their time to the Lord. Well, think about that: the only way someone can give time to God is if that person has enough income or money in the bank so that he or she can take time off work to do the things of God. Most employers will not let you make phone calls to neighbors to invite them to church, go knock on doors, or plan a Bible study on their company time! God can only work through us on this earth, but we cannot finance His kingdom and His work if we do not have the funds. Our enemy, Satan, has arranged the world's system to allow you to have just enough money to get by.

Most people still struggle from paycheck to paycheck, but a surplus is needed to do the job the way God wants it done.

We have already seen that He has put all the wealth in this world that will ever be here. When you put a pan of water on the stove, it doesn't automatically boil. There are certain things you must do to have boiling water—it's obvious, but you need to have a pan of some sort and a heat source, and then you must turn on the heat source. You need to find out what God requires of you, then get in line with that, being obedient to it. So, in a fashion, prosperity is the natural result and outcome of following the Word. You cannot allow other people to deter you from accomplishing your goal.

When the FaithDome was under construction, there was contention from all quarters. Some people said, "You spend all that money on that great big building. Think about the hungry folk out there. You're right in the middle of the ghetto and you spent all that money on a building. How many people could you have fed for what you spent on that?"

If you allow your human feelings to direct your actions, rather than the Lord, it is easy to get caught up in such reasoning. But the minute you do that, you compromise your assignment and the anointing lifts off. At that point, you're back to being on your own, trying to do things on your own strength and ability.

It cost a lot of money to build the FaithDome. We could have taken the $12 million and bought food for the hungry and fed them a few excellent meals. Then what? When those meals were over, they would be hungry again and the $12 million would have been gone. I believe in feeding the hungry. But this is God's business, and ministers make a mistake when they mix up personal feelings for the things of God, attempting to use God's resources to meet what they want to do. That is a trap, because God is about much bigger things than just feeding a few hungry people. God has far more resources than Fred Price does. He knows all about starving people, and you could say He isn't lifting a finger to do anything for them. Why not tell God He is unrighteous or uncaring?

The fact is, there is a reason most of these people are starving, and if you never deal with the reason, they will starve for as long as they live. For the most part, the central reason they are starving is that they do not know Jesus as their Savior and Lord. They do not know that God has a plan for their prosperity and can release them from the bondage of poverty. Salvation is freely offered to us. We just have to receive it by faith. But getting the message of salvation to people, along with teaching them about the victorious lifestyle in Christ that accompanies it, costs a lot of money.

GOD'S PLAN WAS IN ACTION FROM THE BEGINNING

We begin to see God's plan with Abraham. In Genesis 12:1–2, God said to Abram, as he was then called:

> Get out of your country, From your family, And from your father's house, To a land that I will show you. I will make you a great nation; I will bless you And make your name great; And you shall be a blessing.

God started to outline the new system to Abram: "I give you a command, and if you are obedient, I will reward you." In verse 4 of the same chapter, we see that "Abram departed as the LORD had spoken to him." Furthermore, we see that this blessing would not be limited to Abraham. Paul tells us in Galatians that one of the reasons Jesus was crucified was so that the "blessing of Abraham might come upon [us] the Gentiles," and that we might "receive the promise of the Spirit through faith":

> Christ has redeemed us from the curse of the law, having become a curse for us (for it is written, "Cursed is everyone who hangs on a tree"), that the blessing of Abraham might come upon the Gentiles in Christ Jesus, that we might receive the promise of the Spirit through faith.
>
> —Galatians 3:13–14

The new system, then, was a faith-based system, not a labor-based system, and it is available to Christians—to believers, as Galatians 3:9 tells us:

> So then those who are of faith are blessed with believing Abraham.

Blessed *with* him. You might put it, "So then those who are of faith are blessed [along with, in addition to, and *just like*] believing Abraham." That means one of the first things we must do to understand God's plan for prosperity is to examine just how Abraham was blessed. Before we can do that, it is necessary to understand how Abraham could *not* be blessed. Abraham could not be blessed spiritually because Abraham, like Adam after his sin, and like every other man, was reckoned by God to be spiritually dead. Paul says in Romans 5:14, "Nevertheless death reigned from Adam to Moses, even over those who had not sinned according to the likeness of the transgression of Adam." In other words, even those people who had not willfully violated a commandment from God—as Adam had—were "dead." In Romans 8:2 Paul wrote of the "law of sin and death." He said in Romans 5:15 that "by the one man's [Adam] offense many died." Certainly sin brought physical death over time—Adam before the sin did not have to fear physical death so long as he remained in God's will—but that's not what Paul is discussing here. After Adam's offense, which Paul referred to, "many died." We died spiritually. Jesus said that whoever heard His words "has passed from death into life" (John 5:24–25). "Most assuredly, I say to you," Jesus said in verse 25, "the hour is coming, and now is, when the dead will hear the voice of the Son of God; and those who hear will live."

In other words, after Adam's sin, spiritual death was the normal condition of man. As a spiritually dead man, Abraham *could not be blessed spiritually.* (Nor, for that matter, could Noah and his sons in Genesis 9:1. That blessing was a physical blessing on Noah.) Instead, Abraham, Noah, and anyone else who lived before Jesus died for our sins and was resurrected was spiritually dead, and as such could only be blessed in material things. What God did is *account* to them righteousness and spiritual life through their works and obedience. We see in Hebrews 11:7, "By faith Noah, being divinely warned of things not yet seen, moved with godly fear, prepared an ark for the saving of his household, by which he condemned the world and became heir of the righteousness which is according to faith." Likewise, Paul says of Abraham in Romans 4:22 that "it was accounted to him for righteousness." In other words, Noah, Abraham, Enoch, and Elijah did not *have* any righteousness, but God *accounted* it to them for their faith.

I use this example frequently: imagine you are speeding down an interstate and a highway patrol pulls you over and tells you that you were going ninety in a sixty-five-miles per hour zone. He writes the ticket, but then he pulls out his own checkbook, writes out the payment for the fine, and mails it in! You were guilty. You had broken the law. In that case, you were "unrighteous." When the highway patrol paid your penalty, he satisfied the penalty for breaking the law (your sin). That is what Jesus did for us. We don't *have* any righteousness on our own, but we *are* righteousness because Jesus has paid for the cost of our sins and God has accounted it to our ledger. When God looks at you or me, He doesn't see the sinful you or me—He sees the sinless Lamb of God, Jesus.

OLD COVENANT BLESSINGS WERE MATERIAL BLESSINGS

Prior to Jesus coming, men were spiritually dead. God would account to them righteousness for their obedience to the Law. After all, it would have been unjust for God to say, "You are sinful, but Jesus won't be here for one thousand years, so go to hell!" Instead, God said, in essence, "Jesus won't be here for one thousand years, but in the meantime, if you *behave* according to My Law, I'll treat it as though the debt of sin is paid."

Meanwhile, what about the blessing? What about the covenant with Abraham? If Abraham was spiritually dead, how could God bless him? God could bless him materially because Abraham could act in faith in the material world. So we see in Genesis 13:1–2:

> Then Abram [note he was still called "Abram," not "Abraham," which includes the Hebrew word for "God" inserted in Abraham's name, literally meaning "God and Abram"] went up from Egypt, he and his wife and all that he had, and Lot with him, to the South. Abram was very rich in livestock, in silver, and in gold.

In fact, we see in Genesis 13:6: "Now the land was not able to support them [Abram and Lot], that they might dwell together, for their possessions were so great that they could not dwell together." Say what? Their *possessions* were so great they couldn't live in the same area. That must be a lot of possessions. Or, we could say in our modern jargon, "Man, they had a ton of stuff!"

A trend in many modern homes is to have a three-car garage. I remember growing up when many people didn't even have a garage—the fortunate ones had a carport—and a two-car garage was something of a luxury. Today, it's common to have a three-car garage, and the upper-scale homes now have *four*-car garages. Why in the world would you need a three-car garage? Obviously, you would need a three-car garage if you had three cars. If you have so many cars, lawn equipment, bicycles, and extra "stuff" that a two-car garage won't hold it, you need a bigger garage. Abram and Lot needed a bigger garage. They had so many possessions, especially cattle, sheep, and livestock, that it was becoming a problem. We see in 13:7 that strife erupted between their employees, and in verse 8 "Abram said to Lot, 'Please let there be no strife between you and me, and between my herdsmen and your herdsmen; for we are brethren.'"

Abram then gave Lot his choice of the land and said, in essence, "I'll take whatever is left."

How much was that?

> And the LORD said to Abram, after Lot had separated from him; "Lift your eyes now and look from the place where you are—northward, southward, eastward, and westward; for all the land which you see I give to you and your descendants forever. And I will make your descendants as the dust of the earth; so that if a man

could number the dust of the earth, then your descendants also could be numbered."

—Genesis 13:14–16

There are a couple of interesting points here. Note that Abram was *already blessed* before this episode, so much so that he would be, in modern parlance, a millionaire. But after doing the right thing by staying out of strife and giving Lot his choice of the land, God turned him into a "super-millionaire." However, notice also that not one time does God say anything about spiritual blessings, "eternal peace," or anything that could be misconstrued to mean anything other than physical, material blessings.

God continued in this mode, saying "I will make you exceedingly fruitful; and I will make nations of you, and kings shall come from you" (Gen. 17:6). More blessings on old Abe are proclaimed by "the Angel of the LORD," usually a code term for the pre-incarnate Jesus Christ, in Genesis 16:7, 9, 10; then in Genesis 24:35, Abraham's servant (his name was now Abraham) says to Laban, Rebekah's brother, "The LORD has blessed my master greatly, and he has become great; and He has given him flocks and herds, silver and gold, male and female servants, and camels and donkeys." Jacob, Abraham's grandson, "became exceedingly prosperous, and had large flocks, female and male servants, and camels and donkeys" (Gen. 30:43). Not just prosperous—God made him *exceedingly* prosperous. Later on, Laban tells Jacob, Abraham's grandson, "I have learned by experience that the LORD has blessed me for your sake" (Gen. 30:27). Here we have people (first, Lot, then Laban) being blessed just for hanging around those who are righteous!

Abraham's covenant with God had made him and his descendants prosperous in material ways. Yet it wasn't until later with Moses that the specifics of the blessings were enumerated. In Deuteronomy 28, Moses recorded the blessings of obedience:

> Now it shall come to pass, if you [Hebrews] diligently obey the voice of the LORD your God, to observe carefully all His commandments which I command you today, that the LORD your God will set you high above all nations of the earth. And all these blessings...
>
> —Deuteronomy 28:1–2

Right here, to reinforce this, you should say *all* aloud!

> And all these blessings shall come upon you and overtake you, because you obey the voice of the LORD your God; Blessed shall you be in the city, and blessed shall you be in the country. Blessed shall be the fruit of your body, the produce of your ground and the increase of your herds, the increase of your cattle and the offspring of your flocks. Blessed shall be your basket and your kneading bowl. Blessed shall you be when you come in, and blessed shall you be when you go out. The LORD will cause your enemies who rise against you to be defeated before your face; they shall come out against you one way and flee before you seven ways. The LORD will command the blessing on you in your storehouses and in all to which you set your hand, and He will bless you in the land which the LORD your God is giving you.
>
> —Deuteronomy 28:2–8

Then jump to verse 11:

> And the LORD will grant you plenty of goods, in the fruit of your body, in the increase of your livestock, and

in the produce of your ground, in the land of which the LORD swore to your fathers to give you. The LORD will open to you His good treasure, the heavens, to give the rain to your land in its season, and to bless all the work of your hand. You shall lend to many nations, but you shall not borrow. And the LORD will make you the head and not the tail; you shall be above only, and not be beneath, if you heed the commandments of the LORD your God, which I command you today, and are careful to observe them.

—Deuteronomy 28:11–13

For now, I want to postpone the discussion of what these verses may mean for Christians. For Abraham, it's hard to misinterpret this. Someone has to pay you to mess this one up. There is not one single "spiritual" blessing mentioned here. Every one of the blessings mentioned in the verses that we deal with here are material and physical blessings: flocks, baskets, storehouses, kneading bowls, the produce of the ground, and fruit of your body. These were physical and material blessings because, I repeat, until Jesus came, the Jews were spiritually dead and could not be blessed spiritually. The only way God could bless them was materially.

What happened to the Jews when they came out of Egypt? Exodus 12 says that after the Passover, when the Egyptians learned their lesson:

The children of Israel had done according to the word of Moses, and they had asked the Egyptians articles of silver, articles of gold, and clothing. And the LORD had given the people favor in the sight of the Egyptians, so that they granted them what they requested. Thus they plundered the Egyptians.

—Exodus 12:35–36

This doesn't mean the children of Israel ransacked the Egyptians' houses, but that when it was over, it was as if the Hebrews had conquered them. So the Jews left with a great deal of the wealth of Egypt.

Think about this: God knew that the Jews were going to be disobedient. He knew they were going to be walking around the wilderness for forty years. How much good do you think gold and silver did them in the wilderness? Not much. They were worried about getting enough food and water. I'm sure after a while some of them began to wonder why they were even toting around all this heavy metal. There was a purpose.

When Moses built the tabernacle, he spoke to all the congregation, saying, "This is the thing which the LORD commanded, saying: 'Take from among you an offering to the LORD. Whoever is of a willing heart, let him bring it as an offering to the LORD: gold, silver, and bronze,'" as well as many other goods and products (Exod. 35:4–5). Now we see the purpose for why they had gold and silver when they left Egypt—to build the tabernacle. Note however that God did not require them to give up all their gold or silver, but left them plenty after they gave.

This is one of those times when the Jews were being obedient to the Lord, so they gave:

> Then all the craftsmen who were doing all the work of the sanctuary came, each from the work he was doing, and they spoke to Moses, saying, "The people bring much more than enough for the service of the work which the LORD commanded us to do." So Moses gave a commandment...saying, "Let neither man nor woman do any more work for the offering of the sanctuary." And the people were restrained from bringing,

for the material they had was sufficient for all the work to be done—indeed too much.

—Exodus 36:4–7

Look at what the Bible says about David in 1 Chronicles 29:26–28:

Thus David the son of Jesse reigned over all Israel. And the period that he reigned over Israel was forty years; seven years he reigned in Hebron, and thirty-three years he reigned in Jerusalem. So he died in a good old age, full of days and riches and honor; and Solomon his son reigned in his place.

We see, then, that David was "full of riches." What about Solomon?

On that night God appeared to Solomon, and said to him, "Ask! What shall I give you?" And Solomon said to God, "You have shown great mercy to David my father, and have made me king in his place. Now, O LORD God, let Your promise to David my father be established, for You have made me king over a people like the dust of the earth in multitude. Now give me wisdom and knowledge, that I may go out and come in before this people; for who can judge this great people of yours?" Then God said to Solomon: "Because this was in your heart, and you have not asked riches or wealth or honor or the life of your enemies, nor have you asked long life—but have asked wisdom and knowledge for yourself, that you may judge My people over whom I have made you king—wisdom and knowledge are granted to you; and I will give you riches and wealth and honor, such as none of the kings have had who were before you, nor shall any after you have the like."

—2 Chronicles 1:7–12

Solomon did not ask something for himself, but something that would benefit God's people. He "sought first the kingdom of God and His righteousness" and the rest was added to him. (See Matthew 6:33.)

GOD DEALS WITH MAN
ON A PROGRESSIVE BASIS

God has dealt with man on a progressive basis since the fall of Adam. Notice that the Law was not instituted immediately, and Jesus was not born the day after Adam and Eve were booted out of the Garden of Eden. Whenever you want to apply scripture as a proof text for anything, you need to find out if a) it was written for all men, at all times, or a specific group at a specific time, and b) if it was written to a specific group, what group is it? Some truths have universal application, and fit any believer at any time in human history. Consider Psalm 91:1–7:

> He who dwells in the secret place of the Most High Shall abide under the shadow of the Almighty. I will say of the LORD, "He is my refuge and my fortress; My God, in Him I will trust." Surely He shall deliver you from the snare of the fowler And from the perilous pestilence. He shall cover you with His feathers, And under His wings you shall take refuge; His truth shall be your shield and buckler. You shall not be afraid of the terror by night, Nor of the arrow that flies by day, Nor of the pestilence that walks in darkness, Nor of the destruction that lays waste at noonday. A thousand

may fall at your side, And ten thousand at your right hand; But it shall not come near you.

Then, jumping down to verse 16, God says, "With long life I will satisfy him, And show him My salvation."

A devout Jew prior to the coming of Jesus—such as David, who wrote this psalm—could believe this with confidence. Why? Because a Jew would know the Law according to Deuteronomy 28, that he was "blessed in the city, and blessed in the country." He would know that his enemies would come at him from one direction and go away fleeing in seven. David understood his covenant with God and could believe God that even if ten thousand fell all around him, he would be safe. But this psalm is for a Christian, too. Nothing about the Resurrection has changed the part about God being our "shield and buckler" or about not fearing the "terror by night." It is quite the contrary. Because of Jesus we know that our prayers are heard and answered, and that, as Paul says, we are "more than conquerors" (Romans 8:37). Psalm 91, then, is a good example of a universal scripture that applies to us as born-again believers.

The Levitical code, however, is a good example of commandments that were given to specific people (the Jews) at a specific time (until the Messiah came). For one thing, men had to be circumcised under the Law—yet the Jerusalem Council, through the guidance of the Holy Spirit, proclaimed that circumcision was no longer necessary. (See Acts 15:23–29.) Peter, as recorded in Acts 10:9–16, learns that all foods are approved for eating and that a Jew is no longer prohibited from social interactions with Gentiles. Likewise, early in Acts, we see an example of where the Jerusalem church members agree, without any instructions from the Holy Spirit, to engage in a communal economy. They chose to do that, but that was not established as a model for how Church economics were supposed to work.

It is therefore imperative that we as believers "rightly divide" scripture, as Paul told Timothy (2 Tim. 2:15). We need to know what is relevant for us today, and what is not. The Ten Commandments are not for the church today. Jesus said there were only two commandments under the new covenant: to love the Lord your God with all your heart, with all your mind, with all your soul, with all your might, and then to love your neighbor as yourself. (See Mark 12:28–30.) "Thou shalt not steal" is redundant if I am operating in the commandment to love my neighbor, because I would never steal from someone I love. It's worth repeating once more that under the old covenant men were spiritually dead, and therefore they could love one another only with a human kind of love that says "I will love you if you will love me." It amounted to, "I will love you as long as you are pretty, or healthy, or rich." A spiritually dead person could not be expected to love his neighbor unconditionally, especially if his neighbor hated him. He simply wouldn't have the power to love like God.

We Christians, however, can be expected to operate in this higher law of love because we have the Holy Spirit and the love of Christ. "I can do all things through Christ who strengthens me," Paul told the Philippians (4:13). How can you do all things, Paul? Only through Jesus Christ. As with any of God's laws, we must be operating within spiritual and physical laws. Therefore, "I can do all things." This does not mean if you are five feet two inches tall, you can go out for the NBA and dunk a basketball because "Christ strengthens you." There are physical laws in operation. However, let's say you were a five–feet-two-inch-tall person witnessing to people and some unbeliever came after you and you had to run; if the only way for you to escape was to hurdle a wall, God would give you the strength for that—*if* God had called you to be in that situation. The point is, Jesus Christ empowers us to do what He calls us to do—we will see later He never instructed anyone to do anything He didn't do Himself. Jesus called us to love one another, and He has made it possible to love one another by empowering us with His love.

So if the Ten Commandments are not for the church today, what about tithing? Many people want to get out of tithing because they think it was only required under the old covenant. Is it? We will take that up in the next chapter.

Notes

Notes

Chapter 3
THE LAW OF TITHES AND OFFERINGS

I N PREVIOUS CHAPTERS, we have seen how prosperous Abraham was, along with many other servants of God under the old covenant. We have also seen what material blessings that God said He would provide for those who harkened to His Word. Then we examined the laws that apply to us today, contrasted with those that were intended only for certain groups, such as the Jews. What we need to do at this point is to go on a journey through both the Old and New Testament and examine the concept of tithing.

Tithing remains one of those principles that people feel free to take or leave, as though it were a suggestion. One of the most common statements you will hear people make about tithing is, Tithing was under the old covenant and we are not bound by that. By this, people mean that they think tithing was part of the Mosaic Law. In fact, tithing pre-dated the Mosaic Law by four hundred years.

We find that Abram *tithed* long before the Law and the blessings and curses proclaimed in Deuteronomy were ever given. Indeed, the tithe is one of the earliest forms of worship instituted in the Bible. It is introduced completely apart from other codes of law. I think we can assume it's a pretty important principle then. In Genesis 14:18–20 we find:

> Then Melchizedek king of Salem brought out bread and wine; he was the priest of God Most High. And he blessed him [Abram] and said: "Blessed be Abram

of God Most High, Possessor of heaven and earth;
And blessed be God Most High, Who delivered your
enemies into your hand." And he [Abram] gave him
[Melchizedek] a tithe of all.

If you look at the margin notes in the New King James
Bible, you'll see a number next to the word *tithe* that corre-
sponds to a note that says "one-tenth."

Who exactly this Melchizedek was remains a mystery.
Other than Paul's reference to him thousands of years later in
the book of Hebrews, he isn't mentioned again. Here is what
Paul wrote of Jesus and Melchizedek in Hebrews 6:19–20:

This hope we have as an anchor of the soul, both sure
and steadfast, and which enters the Presence behind
the veil [i.e., God], where the forerunner has entered
for us, even Jesus, having become High Priest forever
according to the order of Melchizedek.

It's interesting, just in passing, that the priestly order was
not the order of Melchizedek, but the order of Levi! Here,
Jesus is likened to a priestly order in which there was only
one other such priest—a priest who mysteriously operated
much like Jesus Himself! Paul explains this:

For this Melchizedek, king of Salem, *priest of the Most
High God.*
—Hebrews 7:1, emphasis added

Here we see that phrase used again, when priests came
from the Levites and kings came from the tribe of Judah!
Melchizedek is described as both a king and priest, the only
person in the Old Testament to simultaneously hold that

position other than David (who, in 1 Samuel 21:4–6, ate the showbread, which was reserved for priests only).

Let's go back to Hebrews 7:1–10:

> For this Melchizedek, king of Salem, priest of the Most High God, who met Abraham returning from the slaughter of the kings and blessed him, to whom also Abraham gave a tenth part of all, first being translated "king of righteousness," and then also king of Salem, meaning "king of peace," without father, without mother, without genealogy, having neither beginning of days nor end of life, but made like the Son of God, remains a priest continually. Now consider how great this man was, to whom even the patriarch Abraham gave a tenth of the spoils. And indeed those who are of the sons of Levi, who receive the priesthood, have a commandment to receive tithes from the people according to the law, that is, from their brethren, though they have come from the loins of Abraham; but he whose genealogy is not derived from them received tithes from Abraham and blessed him who had the promises. Now beyond all contradiction the lesser is blessed by the better. Here mortal men receive tithes, but there he receives them, of whom it is witnessed that he lives. Even Levi, who receives tithes, paid tithes through Abraham, so to speak, for he was still in the loins of his father when Melchizedek met him.

Jesus took on the role Melchizedek foreshadowed. Indeed, Paul says in Hebrews 7:11 that a new priesthood was needed:

> Therefore, if perfection were through the Levitical priesthood … what further need was there that another priest should rise according to the order of Melchizedek, and not be called according to the order of Aaron?

Jesus became our High Priest, according to David's prophecy in Psalm 110:4: "You are a priest forever according to the order of Melchizedek." Melchizedek, who foreshadowed Jesus, received the law of tithing, and now Jesus, our great High Priest, administers our current tithes. The tithe did not disappear with the Old Testament any more than the priesthood disappeared. Rather, an imperfect priesthood, that of the Levites, was replaced by the one perfect High Priest, Jesus Christ.

We find the tithe mentioned again in Genesis 28:15–22, where the Lord is speaking of Jacob:

> "Behold, I am with you and will keep you wherever you go, and will bring you back to this land; for I will not leave you until I have done what I have spoken to you." Then Jacob awoke from his sleep and said, "Surely the LORD is in this place, and I did not know it." And he was afraid and said, "How awesome is this place! This is none other than the house of God, and this is the gate of heaven!" Then Jacob rose early in the morning, and took the stone that he had put at his head, set it up as a pillar, and poured oil on top of it. And he called the name of that place Bethel; but the name of that city had been Luz previously. Then Jacob made a vow, saying, "If God will be with me, and keep me in this way that I am going, and give me bread to eat and clothing to put on, so that I come back to my father's house in peace, then the LORD shall be my God, And this stone which I have set as a pillar shall be God's house, and of all that You give me I will surely give a tenth to you."

Here we have Jacob reaffirming the tithe—a tenth—as the norm for obedience. We have seen both Abraham and Jacob blessed lavishly. How do you think they came to be blessed so much? Do you think the fact that they both were obedient in paying their tithe had something to do with it?

The next time the tithe is specifically discussed is in Malachi, the last book before the arrival of Christ. Malachi begins chapter three (recognizing that chapter and verse designations were only added by the translators hundreds of years later) with the proclamation that a messenger, whom we now know was John the Baptist would prepare the way for the Messiah. The Lord, through the prophet, soon moves into a remonstrance of the Jews for their disobedience:

> "Yet from the days of your fathers You have gone away from My ordinances and have not kept them. Return to Me, and I will return to you," says the Lord of hosts. "But you said, 'In what way shall we return?' Will a man rob God? Yet you have robbed Me! But you say, 'In what way have we robbed You?' In tithes and offerings. You are cursed with a curse, For you have robbed Me, Even this whole nation. Bring all the tithes into the storehouse, That there may be food in My house, And try Me now in this," says the LORD of hosts, "If I will not open for you the windows of heaven And pour out for you such blessing That there will not be room enough to receive it. And I will rebuke the devourer for your sakes, So that he will not destroy the fruit of your ground, Nor shall the vine fail to bear fruit for you in the field," says the LORD of hosts.
>
> —Malachi 3:7–11

Again, some people think tithing originated here in Malachi. No! Tithing is first recorded in Genesis. We see it again and again throughout the Old Testament.

Rather, in Malachi, God is rebuking the Israelites for *failing* to tithe, and reminding them that He wanted them to return to their former obedience and faithfulness, as demonstrated by Abraham and Jacob. Malachi 3:10 is quoted frequently, especially when churches need to meet their budgets. But look at 3:3–5 to put this in context:

> He [God] will sit as a refiner and a purifier of silver; He will purify the sons of Levi, And purge them as gold and silver, that they may offer to the LORD an offering in righteousness. "Then the offering of Judah and Jerusalem Will be pleasant to the LORD, As in the days of old, As in former years. And I will come near you for judgment; I will be a swift witness Against sorcerers, Against adulterers, Against perjurers, Against those who exploit wage earners and widows and orphans, And against those who turn away an alien—Because they do not fear Me," says the LORD of hosts.

In this passage, God is exhorting the Levites regarding the sacrifices for sin. The Levites were priests, those charged with the responsibility of making the sacrifices to atone for sin, and therefore the whole discussion of tithing is placed in the broader context of obedience to the Lord. God says when the people obeyed Him, He would take action against those who afflicted His people.

We will later examine how some of these things specifically relate to Christians, but what I want you to see here is that tithing was instituted long before the Law; that the "big names" of the Old Testament, including Abraham and Jacob, tithed, and that God reprimanded the Jews when they got away from tithing.

I have repeatedly agreed with critics of tithing that we are no longer under the Law. But that is irrelevant when it comes to tithing because tithing is a law beyond the Ten Commandments and even the broader "commandments" that Jesus refers to on many occasions. It is a law of God in the same way that gravity is a law—it is a universal principle.

TITHING WORKS...FOR EVERYONE

Understand that *God does not need your money*. We already established in chapter one that He is rich beyond all comprehension. He invented the wealth, after all! So this universal principle, this law of tithing, was instituted *for all mankind!* If you get in the flow of how God's Word operates, it will work for you. When you turn on the water in your shower, you will not get a drop of that water on you, even if you walk around outside all day, until you get in the shower. Then you will get wet because that is where the water is falling. God's blessings are like that falling water. If you want to get wet, you have to get in the water. Look at someone like John D. Rockefeller, one of the richest men in America in the 1800s. His ledgers show that by the age of sixteen, before he had much income, he was tithing consistently *and* giving to charities. At age twenty-one, he successfully raised two thousand dollars (or about forty-five thousand dollars in modern money) to pay the church's lease. Concerned that he couldn't pay proper attention to giving, he hired someone to supervise his philanthropy![1]

Many years ago I was broke all the time. I couldn't afford clothes for the children, could barely keep a car running, had a house that you could practically extend both arms and touch both sides of the house. Our struggles had struggles. And yet the blessings were available, all the time. I just wasn't in them. The water was running, and I was outside the shower. God will not bring His laws into line with your behavior, actions, and confessions. You must bring your behavior, actions, and confessions in line with His laws.

The law of tithing is simple. Malachi 3:10 says, "Bring all the tithes into the storehouse... [and God will] open for you the windows of heaven And pour out for you such blessing That there will not be room enough to receive it." Let's break that down. The verse starts with the phrase, "Bring all." In other words, if you aren't bringing a full 10 percent of your earnings, you are not bringing all. You may be bringing 3 percent, 5 percent, or 9 percent, in which case you are only partially obedient—which is to say, you are in disobedience. If you tell your child to clean up his room and you come in a half hour later and it's all clean except that all his things are thrown under the bed, then it isn't clean. The child has not been obedient.

What constitutes 10 percent? It's not as easy a question as you might think, given our modern systems of taxation and "forced" contribution, such as Social Security. Some people suggest that you need to give 10 percent of your gross pay. But you have no control over how those forced taxes are spent or whether or not you contribute to unemployment or Social Security. You are welcome to tithe off the gross if you like, but I believe God expects us to give from what we control, which truly shows where our priorities are. So from my perspective, tithing off the net (after taxes and forced contributions) is biblical. Of course, that would not include personal funds that you decide to save, or put in special funds as automatic payroll deductions.

The best rule is to be honest. You know if you are "shuckin' and jivin'" the Lord, and He knows it too. He also knows if you are honestly doing everything you can to tithe. This is where tithing can get into religious ritual, much like the

Pharisees counting their grains of salt. How silly is that? If you are really concerned, give just a little more than you think is 10 percent and you'll never have a problem.

So we've established *what* to give—what it is that constitutes the tithe. Offerings are over and above the tithe. Say you make two thousand dollars every two weeks at your job, and you write a check to your church for two hundred dollars every payday. That is the minimum. That is your basic requirement in God's eyes for obedience. Remember, it's not the letter of the law, because as Paul told us the letter of the law kills, but the spirit gives life. (See 2 Corinthians 3:6.) You are writing that check because you love the Lord. You *want* to be obedient. However, because you love Him, you decide to send fifty dollars for that African missions trip or give to a hurricane relief fund. That is terrific. Those are *offerings*. God loves them, so long as they are made with a willing and generous heart. However, do not think because you wrote a check to the Salvation Army or to the Red Cross that you have tithed. No!

The reason is clear: if you look at the next phrase in Malachi 3:10, you can see that God tells you how the tithe is to be paid: "Bring all the tithes into the storehouse." The storehouse is the church. Jesus said in Matthew 6:21, "For where your treasure is, there your heart will be also." One way God has of building support for His local churches is through the tithe. Colleges and universities have known this for years: if you can get alumni to give to the school, they become much more emotionally attached to that college or university. They start attending speeches, sporting events, and art exhibits there. Your heart follows your wallet. This is why it is important for us to confess God's Word and follow through with our actions to re-shape our hearts. God is a lot smarter than we are. Romans 4:17 says God "gives life to the dead and calls those things which do not exist as though they did." What you begin to confess with your mouth and do with your actions will change your behavior.

How to Tithe—Don't "Mail It In"

You should bring the tithes into the church. Do not send them in. Obviously, if you are out of town on business, it's legitimate to send in a tithe. It should not become a habit whereby you say, "I'll just send in a check," yet never go personally to the storehouse to worship with your tithes. Your heart won't change if you don't bring the tithe into the storehouse. Paul, in 2 Corinthians 9:7, wrote: "So let each one give as he purposes in his heart, not grudgingly or of necessity; for God loves a cheerful giver." That word *cheerful* can be translated "happy" or even "hilarious." Paul was telling us that if you are begrudging your giving, then it isn't a gift at all. At Crenshaw Christian Center, we acknowledge our deliverance from poverty when we present our tithes and offerings by holding up our offering envelopes, as if placing them in the hands of Jesus. While we do this, we make this confession of faith:

> Heavenly Father, we profess this day to You that we have come into the inheritance which You swore to give us. We are in the land which You have provided for us in Jesus Christ, the kingdom of Almighty God. We were sinners serving Satan; he was our god, but we called upon the name of Jesus and You heard our cry and delivered us from the power of darkness and translated us into the kingdom of Your dear Son.

Jesus, as our Lord and High Priest, we bring the firstfruits of our income to You, that You may worship the Lord our God with them. Father, we rejoice in all the good which You have given to us and to our households. We have heard Your voice and have done according to all that You have commanded us.

Now Father, as You look down from Your holy habitation from heaven to bless us as You said in Your Word, we believe that we now receive those blessings according to Your Word. This is our confession of faith, in Jesus' name. Amen.

We are tailoring our confession for the new covenant dispensation. We don't just do this to fill up time, and we don't just stuff money into an envelope. Our tithing is a part of our worship.

Remember, *God doesn't need your money.* When the basket comes around, you ought to have such joy in your heart that you break out into applause or laughter at the great blessings God is about to pour out on you!

Note what Paul says right after telling you to give "cheerfully" or "hilariously": "And God is able to make all grace abound toward you, that you, always having all sufficiency in all things, may have an abundance for every good work" (2 Cor. 9:8). That sounds to me like a result of giving will be "always having all sufficiency in all things," and having more than enough ("an abundance") for every good work.

Why does tithing produce prosperity? Tithing, obviously, is an act of obedience, and God loves obedience. On the other hand, He looks at going through the motions of obedience as "smoke in My nostrils," a sacrifice without meaning

(Isa. 65:5). "Behold, to obey is better than sacrifice, And to heed than the fat of rams" wrote Samuel (1 Sam. 15:22). Tithing as an act of obedience is worship and pleasing to God. However, tithing in hopes of "buying God off" or tithing *only* in the hope of getting a return are both "smoke in God's nostrils."

In addition to the blessings of obedience, tithing produces prosperity due to the biblical principle of seed-time and harvest. Sometimes Christians get the euphoric idea that things are going to fall out of heaven. God doesn't work like that. Money has to come through the hands of men. If you think about it, even when you had some emergency need, and a check miraculously appeared, that check came from some person, some business, or some agency. Adam handed over all authority over the earth to Satan with his act of rebellion—disobedience. The dominion of the earth passed, in order, from God to Adam to Satan. For God to legally act in this world, He has to act through mankind, who were originally given dominion. Today, most economic circumstances on earth are controlled in one way or another by satanic influence. You don't have to be a devil worshipper for this to be the case: if you are not a co-worker with God—which means you are not one of His children—your earthly activities are already operating under the auspices of "Satan, Inc." As we will see, one of the main purposes of Christians being prosperous is to regain control of the world's wealth out of the hands of the devil. If that were the *only* reason for Christians to be prosperous, it would be enough, but there are many others.

How Tithing Brings Prosperity

So how does tithing work to bring you prosperity? Proverbs 3:9–10 says:

> Honor the LORD with your possessions, And with the firstfruits of all your increase; So your barns will be filled with plenty, And your vats will overflow with new wine.

This is a simple two-part process. The first part is your responsibility: "Honor the LORD with your possessions, And with the firstfruits of all your increase;" and the second part is God's: "So [that] your barns will be filled with plenty, And your vats will overflow with new wine." Most of us today are not farmers, nor do we run vineyards. So another way of reading this for modern times would be, "Give the Lord honor through your possessions by giving Him the first of your profits from your work or business, so that your bank accounts will be large and your stock portfolios will keep on growing." I know some ministers who have a problem with prosperity absolutely cringe when you say something like this, and yet what other message can you take from that if you put it in modern terms?

For your part, you "honor the LORD with your possessions." Remember *all* your possessions are God's. They all came from Him. If He had stopped the verse right there, then we would have a different system to work under, in which you would be expected to give everything you have to the church and let the local minister decide what to let you live on. Since it's all God's anyway, can we agree that, however painful that might be to us, it would be just? Yes, it would. We didn't create the raw materials, the concepts, the talent, or even the energy needed to produce one iota of wealth. God did it all. So He would be perfectly just in demanding it all back. But thank God He doesn't! As we have seen, God only wants 10 percent.

God reaffirmed this promise in Malachi 3:10 where He said, "'And try me now in this,' Says the LORD of hosts, 'If I will not open for you the windows of heaven and pour out for you such blessing that there will not be room enough to receive it.'" God's part is to respond to our giving with a "windows of heaven" blessing that is so intense, so exceptional, we will be in a better position to give even more. Further, He even added in verse 11: "'And I will rebuke the devourer for your sakes, So that he [Satan] will not destroy the fruit of your ground, Nor shall the vine fail to bear fruit for you in the field,' says the LORD of hosts."

Notice that God not only is going to give you material wealth—because for Malachi, who was under the old covenant, there could be no other meaning than physical and material possessions—but God also said He would protect your possessions from the devil. *Did you know that this is the only place in the entire Bible where God said He would do something about the devil?*

Every other reference to believers dealing with Satan requires us to rebuke him, to cast him out, and so on. Every other time, the burden is on us to do something. Look at James 4:7, "Therefore submit to God. Resist the devil and he will flee from you." Paul told the Ephesians to "put on the whole armor of God, that you may be able to stand against the wiles of the devil" (Eph. 6:11). God's instructions to us regarding the devil are to submit to God, resist the devil, put on the whole armor of God, and stand.

Malachi is the one place where God said *He* would take care of the devil for us—when we tithed. To again use our modern vernacular, it is as if God said, "Give the Lord honor through your possessions by giving Him the first of your profits from your work or business, so that your bank accounts will be large and your stock portfolios will keep on growing. *And* I will personally make sure that the devil cannot interfere with your bank accounts or your stock portfolios!" Isn't it interesting that the only place where God says He will fight the devil for us is when it comes to this business of tithing? It must be pretty important, don't you think?

Returning now to the issue of seed-time and harvest, Paul wrote in Galatians 6:7–8:

> Do not be deceived, God is not mocked; for whatever a man sows, that he will also reap. For he who sows to his flesh will of the flesh reap corruption, but he who sows to the Spirit will of the Spirit reap everlasting life.

Some will try to say this tells us *not* to expect physical blessings, but that isn't what this says at all. If you are sowing seed into the kingdom, that *is* a spiritual act, and, yes, you will reap everlasting life. But that's not all you will reap, because Malachi clearly says you will also reap material prosperity beyond all measure.

THE PRINCIPLE OF SOWING AND REAPING

This principle of sowing and reaping is repeated many times in the Bible. Here is another reference in Hosea 8:7 of apostate Israel, "They sow the wind, And reap the whirlwind." Note, though, that whether good or bad, what you reap is always greater than what you sowed! The temporary sowing of flesh will produce eternal reaping of corruption, and the temporary sowing of tithes into God's kingdom will produce everlasting prosperity.

No field will bring forth a crop until the farmer plants seed in it. If the farmer chooses to eat his seed and not plant it, he will be temporarily full, but very quickly he will run out of food for the years to come. Even the minimum wage worker knows that he or she has to put in forty hours first, and then the paycheck comes later. Some businesses do not pay you until you put in two weeks' worth of work.

Perhaps the hardest part of tithing is getting that first check, especially if you have tithed and now have your first return. The human tendency is to say, "OK, now I can pay off all those bills! I'll just skip my tithe this one time, and next time, I can pay it because I won't have any bills." Uh oh. You just prevented God from protecting your seed. Before that next check comes in, your car will break down, you will have an emergency illness, the school will need extra, unexpected money from you for the kids—the devil will *make sure* that you do not have an excess the next time. So you have to start all over again. This is the tough part. Here is where Paul's words about the "whole armor" of God and "standing" come in. Perhaps here, even more than when you first made that commitment to tithe, you have to stand. God cannot stand for you.

Again, we are brought back to the discussion in chapter one about capitalism and investment and the imperative to "give [first], and it will be given to you: good measure, pressed down, shaken together, and running over will be put into your bosom. For with the same measure that you use, it will be measured back to you" (Luke 6:38). This does not mean if you tithe fifty dollars you will get back only fifty dollars. Rather, that seed will be "pressed down, shaken together, and running over." It will be "measured back to you," but not with the same measures *you* used when you measured it out because you measure things in human terms; God measures back to you in His terms!

If you need an example of this, look at the life of Elijah and the widow in 1 Kings 17:8–16:

> Then the word of the LORD came to him [Elijah], saying, "Arise, go to Zarephath, which belongs to Sidon, and dwell there. See, I have commanded a widow there to provide for you." So he arose and went to Zarephath. And when he came to the gate of the city, indeed a widow was there gathering sticks. And he called to her and said, "Please bring me a little water in a cup, that I may drink." And as she was going to get it, he called to her and said, "Please bring me a morsel of bread in your hand." So she said, "As the LORD your God lives, I do not have bread, only a handful of flour in a bin, and a little oil in a jar; and see, I am gathering a couple of sticks that I may go in an prepare it for myself and my son, that we may eat it, and die." And Elijah said to her, "Do not fear; go and do as you have said, but make me a small cake from it first, and bring it to me; and afterward make some for yourself and your son. For thus says the LORD God of Israel: 'The bin of flour shall not be used up, nor shall the jar of oil run dry, until the day the LORD sends rain on the earth.'" So she went away and did according to the word of Elijah; and she and he and her household ate for many days. The bin of flour was not used up, nor did the jar of oil run dry, according to the word of the LORD which He spoke by Elijah.

This incident did not involve tithing, but it involved two of the key principles of tithing—obedience and "give and it shall be given." Notice that the woman, who no doubt was hungry herself and had a hungry son to feed, had just enough flour for two people to eat. If she gave it to Elijah and he decided to eat both pieces, neither she nor her son would have anything to eat. It was a great risk. Yet she was obedient to the Word of the Lord and gave Elijah the first cake. Then the Word of the Lord came to pass, and "the bin of flour was not used up, nor did the jar of oil run dry" (v. 16).

In 2 Kings 4:1–7 we see a similar demonstration of the same principles of obedience and giving with Elisha:

> A certain woman of the wives of the sons of the prophets cried out to Elisha, saying, "Your servant my husband is dead, and you know that your servant feared the LORD. And the creditor is coming to take my two sons to be his slaves." So Elisha said to her, "What shall I do for you? Tell me, what do you have in the house?" And she said, "Your maidservant has nothing in the house but a jar of oil." Then he said, "Go, borrow vessels from everywhere, from all your neighbors—empty vessels; do not gather just a few. And when you have come in, you shall shut the door behind you and your sons; then pour it into all those vessels, and set aside the full ones." So she went from him and shut the door behind her and her sons, who brought the vessels to her; and she poured it out. Now it came to pass, when the vessels were full, that she said to her son, "Bring me another vessel." And he said to her, "There is not another vessel." So the oil ceased. Then she came and told the man of God. And he said, "Go, sell the oil and pay your debt; and you and your sons live on the rest."

Once again we see the principles of obedience, sowing, reaping, and of increase. Elisha did not put a limit on how many vessels she could borrow. In fact, he tried to tip her off by saying, "Do not gather just a few" (v. 3). Elisha knew what was about to happen, and he knew—but couldn't tell her—that every jar she collected would be filled with oil. It was the same principles that God used with Isaac:

> Then Isaac sowed in that land, and reaped in the same year a hundredfold; and the LORD blessed him. The man began to prosper, and continued prospering until he became very prosperous; for he had possessions of flocks and possessions of herds and a great number of servants. So the Philistines envied him.
>
> —Genesis 26:12–14

Isaac reaped in the same year and didn't just get back what he put into the land; he got back a hundredfold. For those determined to miss the message here, God made it impossible to misconstrue this as spiritual blessings because he said "*possessions* of flocks and *possessions* of herds." It's quite clear that Isaac prospered in material blessings.

God told Joshua, "Arise, go over this Jordan, you and all this people, to the land which I am giving them—the children of Israel. Every place that the sole of your foot will tread upon I have given you, as I said to Moses" (Josh. 1:2). What an incredible statement. Joshua had a blank check. Wherever he walked, God already decreed that the land would belong to the Israelites. You'd think old Josh would still be walking today with that kind of a deal.

Some of you will say, "These are all Old Testament examples, so they don't really apply to me today." Hold on! Not so fast! In Luke 5, we see the account of Jesus at the Lake of Gennesaret. He saw fishermen who had already left their boats (we soon learn one of them was Simon Peter), and they were washing their nets. Jesus climbed into Peter's boat, sat down, and started to teach all the people. When He finished His sermon, Jesus said to Peter:

> "Launch out into the deep and let down your nets for a catch." But Simon answered and said to Him, "Master, we have toiled all night and caught nothing; nevertheless at Your word I will let down the net."
> —Luke 5:4–5

This passage is supremely instructive. Peter knew Jesus was Lord. He had seen Him heal the sick, cast out demons, and perform other miracles—although possibly you could argue that this was very early in Jesus ministry and Peter hadn't seen many miracles. Still, Peter's response is so typical of our reply to God most of the time when we are called to do something. We want to remind God how hard *we* have worked, which is totally irrelevant. It doesn't matter how much you toil on something; if God isn't in it, you will have zero returns. Unlike some Christians, at least Peter was obedient in the long run: "Nevertheless at Your word I will let down the net." If most of us get to this point, we would be doing well to be able to say, "Nevertheless, Lord, at Your command I will obey." How much better, though, to be obedient without everything that precedes the "nevertheless"? How much better to obey instantly without reminding God of what hasn't worked before?

When the net started to break, Peter called for help:

> So they signaled to their partners in the other boat to come and help them. And they came and filled both

the boats, so that they began to sink.... For he and all
who were with him were astonished at the catch of fish
which they had taken.

—Luke 5:7, 9

Peter and his business partners had worked all night
and gotten nothing, and in a few minutes, with Jesus, they
caught more fish than they had in the last twenty-four hours.
Jesus gave him a prosperity harvest: good measure, shaken
together, and literally running over.

In all of these examples, we have several common ingredients. God, sometimes through a prophet, sometimes directly,
gave instructions that were open-ended in their outcome.
What the person received was geometrically measured back
based on what they gave in faith. The person's faith tested
not only whether someone was obedient, but to what extent
he or she believed God would provide. The woman with the
pots could have said, "OK, the prophet said to gather more
than a few. Well, I guess a *few* is three or four, so I'll get six.
That should be plenty." We don't know the number she actually got, but clearly it was more than five or six. She not only
had enough to pay off her entire debt, but to "live on the
rest." Do you think if she knew that *any* pot she got would
be filled with oil, she would have gone to surrounding towns
and villages and gotten every pot in the region? I suspect she
would have.

Do you think Joshua walked as much as he possibly
could so that he set foot on as much land as possible? I'm
sure he did. Contrast that with Peter, who let down only
one net. What kind of response do you expect from God
when He commands you to do something? Do you have a
"many vessels" level of faith? Or do you have a "one net"
level of faith?

Your act of faith for God means obedience, but it also demands excellence. Jesus said, "He who is faithful in what is least is faithful also in much; and he who is unjust in what is least is unjust also in much" (Luke 16:10). If you sow with little faith, you will receive a little reward. You will receive something, but it won't be as much as if you sow with great faith.

DO NOT PAY TITHE TO THE DEAD

We have looked earlier at the fact that your heart follows your wallet and that you should bring all the tithes into the storehouse, the storehouse being your local church. But in Deuteronomy 26:14, Moses wrote this of the tithe:

> I have not eaten any of it when in mourning, nor have I removed any of it for an unclean use, nor given any of it for the dead. I have obeyed the voice of the LORD my God, and have done according to all that You have commanded me.

The *Amplified Bible* puts it like this: "Nor given any of it to the dead." What does that mean? It means, first and foremost, that you are responsible for seeing that the tithe gets into a ministry that is about life—teaching God's Word. When I started out as an assistant minister, the pastor of that church was an excellent speaker. But when I look back and examined the content of what he was teaching, it was death. Something can sound good but have no life in it. You need to ask yourself when you go to church, what do you receive? Are you getting the meat of God's Word? If not, then it is a dead church and you have no business giving a tithe to a dead church.

Any church that denies the Holy Spirit in the sanctuary or in the members who come to that sanctuary is a dead church. Zechariah 4:6 says, "'Not by might nor by power, but by My Spirit,' says the LORD of hosts." If the Holy Spirit is not allowed to be part of the service, and if people are denied the right to be filled with the Holy Spirit, as provided under the New Testament, that is a dead church. It may be teaching religious doctrine or denominational theology, but it isn't teaching the Bible. If you place your tithe in a church that doesn't believe in divine health or healing, you will have to give an account to God. Any church that does not pray for the sick is a dead church.

Mark 16:17 records that Jesus Himself said, "And these signs will follow those who believe: In My name they will cast out demons; they will speak with new tongues." So if the signs don't follow, you have to wonder if they really believe in Jesus.

This has nothing to do with the sincerity of people or even their love for Jesus. Plenty of good people love the Lord but just do not know the Word. It doesn't have anything to do with how long you have been attending church. If you are on a U.S. highway and you've been going east for two days hoping to get to Los Angeles, it won't happen—you are going the wrong way. It is time to turn around.

Nor should you divide your tithe. You can only have one storehouse—Jesus said you cannot serve two masters. When you find that church where you are being fed the Word, that is where your tithe should go. If you want to give offerings to other ministries off of the remaining 90 percent of the money that belongs to you, you are free to give that to whomever you want. That is your money to give as an offering—the tithe is not. Further, it is not legitimate to use your tithe to purchase

Christian materials—music, tapes, or even a Bible. The tithe is owed to God and paid to the storehouse, that "there may be food in My house" (Mal. 3:10).

There is also a time to pay up. If you have been robbing God, you can fix this curse. However, like every bank or credit card company you can think of has a late fee for when you miss your payments, so does God. In Leviticus 27:30–31, you see God's penalty for stealing the tithe and robbing God:

And all the tithe of the land, whether of the seed of the land or of the fruit of the tree, is the *Lord's*. It is holy to the Lord. If a man wants at all to redeem any of his tithes, he shall add one-fifth to it.

Say your tithe (10 percent of your income) is ten dollars, but you only give five dollars. You have robbed God of five dollars. So the next time you pay your tithes, instead of the 10 percent you would normally pay, you have to pay the five dollars you did not pay previously, plus a penalty of 20 percent on that five dollars. Your total tithe would be sixteen dollars.

It's so much easier just to develop a mind-set, an attitude toward your income, that already takes into account the tithe. When you see a check for one thousand dollars, think, "I just got a check for nine hundred dollars." Then you won't be as tempted to spend God's money. Again, the devil will immediately come at you with all sorts of great things you can do with that money. When he says that to me, I rebuke him immediately in Jesus' name and say, "If you don't shut up, I'll push my tithe up another 10 percent!" I have not missed a tithe in thirty-three years.

Later, we'll examine how you can get out of financial debt, even when you are in deep financial trouble. God is not without mercy. Meanwhile, purpose in your heart to get in the tithing habit.

Notes

Notes

Chapter 4
A NEW AND BETTER COVENANT

I N THE FIRST chapters, we've seen that God isn't poor—that He not only has all the wealth in the world, but created it in the first place; that the promises of God to Abraham consisted almost entirely of material prosperity and that the only way God could bless man at that time was materially. Abraham ensured his material blessing through the obedience of tithing. We saw that there were spiritual principles—laws—involved in tithing, including the law of seedtime and harvest, and that God considers it robbery when you do not pay the tithe. We also looked at the process by which you tithe and if it is acceptable to pay your tithes to just any church.

So far, we really have not left the Old Testament in terms of principles. The processes that I've outlined here worked for all of the faithful and obedient men and women of the Old covenant. After all, *covenant* means "promise," and the Old Testament, or "old promise," does not mean "defunct" so much as it means "updated, new, and improved with better promises." We call that agreement the New Testament or the new covenant, because Jesus instituted a new, better agreement when He lived, died, and rose from the dead on our behalf.

First, let's establish the fact that God cannot lie. Numbers 23:19 states plainly, "God is not a man, that He should lie." Moreover, when God makes a promise, He cannot break it (again, because He cannot lie). As Psalm 138:2 says, "For You [God] have magnified Your word above all Your name." There are some people who think God can do anything at any time. While technically that is true—He has the *power* to do whatever He wants because He is God—there are several things God can't do. It's common sense. He cannot save you against your will. If you want to go to hell, He must let you. I've used this example in my book, *Answered Prayer Guaranteed!* but it's a good one which I choose to use again. There is a movie called *Bruce Almighty* about a guy named Bruce (played by Jim Carrey) who thinks God is falling down on the job and that he could be a better "God." So God (played by Morgan Freeman) temporarily hands over power to Bruce. Bruce loves a girl named Hope, but manages to mess up their relationship. She leaves him, and in one insightful scene, Bruce asks "God," "How do you get someone to love you without violating free will?" And "God" answers, "Welcome to My world, son!" That's exactly right: God will not make you love Him, and actually He will not make someone else love you—nor will He force anyone to love Jesus. Love must be freely given. That's "God's world."

Well, lying is something else God will not do, because to lie would be to put Him on man's plane and to make Him as changeable and corruptible as man. So when the psalmist says "You have magnified Your word above all Your name," it means that when God promises something, He will not break that promise. It's the most ironclad agreement in the universe. Moreover, we see that God doesn't change: James 1:17, which we looked at earlier in a different context says, "Every good gift and every perfect gift is from above, and comes down from the Father of lights, with whom there is no variation or shadow of turning." That means that God won't do what men do all the time, namely to make an agreement sincerely with all honesty *at the time*, then when circumstances change, think, "Well, things are different now, and I no longer have to live up to that contract." Isn't that how most marriages today end? People say, "He changed," or, "She changed." Well, as the teens say, Duh! Of course people change. Do you really want that twenty-five-year-old boy you married to be acting twenty-five when he is fifty-eight? Do you really want that twenty-two-year-old girl you met still going to the disco when she has three children at home?

People change because we are temporal, and our lives are like a leaf blowing through a yard. But God is eternal. He lives in one permanent present. He has no need to change because He is perfect. And since Jesus is the Son of God, He doesn't change either: Hebrews 13:8 tells us that "Jesus Christ is the same yesterday, today, and forever." That means when Jesus gives us His Word, we can count on it too. He will not lie.

STAY IN LINE WITH GOD'S WILL

Because God is a God of integrity, He chooses not to lie, and the validity of His contract/covenant shows why faith is so essential. To not have faith that God will perform His Word is to call Him a liar. Likewise, to refuse to take Jesus Christ at His Word is to call Him a liar. Faith, or "acting on one's belief," is a physical response to God's spiritual promise. For the blessings of God to manifest in your life, however, not only must you have faith, but it must be faith in line with a promise of God. You cannot just have faith that the Dallas Cowboys will win the Super Bowl next year. You might wish it, but nowhere in the Bible will you find that promised to you. But you *can* find it promised, "Give, and it will be given to you" (Luke 6:38), or "Whatever things you ask when you pray, believe that you receive them, and you will have them" (Mark 11:24). Knowing what is promised, therefore, is absolutely essential to your receiving.

"Well," some people say, "we can't really know what God has planned for us." Then they will cite Isaiah 55:8: "'For My thoughts are not your thoughts, nor are your ways My ways,' says the Lord." Perhaps there is no more abused scripture in the entire Bible than this one. If you look at the context, it makes all the difference in the world. God was not addressing this to believers:

> Seek the LORD while He may be found, Call upon Him while He is near. Let the wicked...
> —Isaiah 55:6–7

Who? "The wicked." Quoting the Lord Jehovah, Isaiah wrote:

> Let the wicked forsake his way, And the unrighteous man...
> —Isaiah 55:7

Who? "The unrighteous man." The rest of the passage continues:

> Let the wicked forsake his way, And the unrighteous man *his thoughts*; let him return to the LORD, And He will have mercy on him; And to our God, For He will abundantly pardon. "For My thoughts are not your thoughts, Nor are your ways My ways," says the LORD, "For as the heavens are higher than the earth, So are My ways higher than your ways, And My thoughts than your thoughts."

Whose thoughts were previously under discussion? According to verse 7, it is the unrighteous man's thoughts. And whose ways were previously under discussion? The wicked man's ways. You have to pay someone to help you misinterpret this. God was not telling Isaiah that no one can know God's thoughts or His ways, only that the "wicked" and the "unrighteous" do not know His ways and thoughts. Well, what do you expect? Wouldn't you as a believer be just a little concerned if the wicked and the unrighteous were on the same wavelength as our Lord?

These verses in Isaiah are telling us that while the wicked and the unrighteous can't know God's thoughts or ways, those faithful to the Lord, even under the old covenant, could.

> So shall My word be that goes forth from My mouth; it shall not return to Me void, But it shall accomplish what I please, And it shall prosper in the thing for which I sent it. "For you [faithful Believer, you who listen to My Word, you who know My thoughts and My ways] shall go out with joy, And be led out with peace; The mountains and the hills shall break forth into singing before you, And all the trees of the field shall clap their hands.
>
> —Isaiah 55:11–12

It is pretty plain that the Word does not return to God void but accomplishes what He pleases, because there are Christians who listen to God's Word and are obedient. Those are the people who know God's ways and understand God's thoughts.

James wrote, "If any of you lacks wisdom"—in other words, if you do not know God's will for a situation—"let him ask of God, who gives to all [Christians] liberally and without reproach, and it will be given to him. But let him ask in faith, with no doubting" (James 1:5–6). Note that James did not say, "If any of you lacks wisdom, your thoughts are not God's thoughts, so abandon any attempt to know His thoughts." No! It tells us clearly that if we seek God, He will give us wisdom and understanding to know His will. There is a catch: "Let him ask in faith, with no doubting" (v. 6). Do you see now why the verses in Isaiah say what they say? The sinner, the non-believer, the unfaithful man cannot know God's thoughts or His ways because he can't even *ask* for understanding *in faith*. The sinner will already have doubt, and so his answer is aborted before the question even gets out of his mouth. Moreover, Hosea 4:6 warns us about the dangers of *not* knowing God's thoughts and ways: "My people are destroyed for lack of knowledge." How unfair of God would it be to on the one hand say, "You idiots are dying because you don't have any knowledge, wisdom, or understanding about My thoughts and ways," then on the other hand turn around and say, "You can't know My thoughts or ways. It's impossible!" Do you see how unjust that would be?

There is still more evidence that we can know God's will. Ephesians 3 begins with Paul explaining, "How that by revelation He made known to me the mystery.... which in other ages was not made known to the sons of men, as it has now been revealed by the Spirit to His holy apostles and prophets" (Eph. 3:3, 5). In other words, Paul explains that there were things he learned, through revelation, that were not known in other ages. Paul goes on to write that he preached Jesus "to make all see what is the fellowship of the mystery, which from the beginning of the ages has been hidden in God who created all things through Jesus Christ; to the intent that now the *manifold wisdom of God might be made known by the church to the principalities and powers in the heavenly places*" (Eph. 3:9–10, emphasis added). So even if it was impossible, prior to Jesus, for faithful men to know the thoughts and ways of God—which is not what is stated in Isaiah—certainly after Jesus is resurrected and Paul has this revelation, the intention of God is that His "manifold wisdom... might be made known by the church" to all. Can we know the thoughts and ways of God? Absolutely.

Paul says in 1 Corinthians 2:7–8: "But we speak the wisdom of God in a mystery, the hidden wisdom which God ordained before the ages for our glory, which none of the rulers of this age knew [referring to the Jewish leaders]; for had they known, they would not have crucified the Lord of glory." So Paul wrote that he and his fellow disciples *back then* had already been given "the wisdom of God in a mystery, the hidden wisdom which God ordained before... for our glory," or before they were alive. God had given Paul the wisdom that He had hidden for centuries, the wisdom about Jesus the Messiah. Obviously, the rulers of the day didn't get it because they crucified Him. Look at what Paul wrote next: "But as it is written: 'Eye has not seen, nor ear heard, Nor have entered into the heart of man The things which God has prepared for those who love Him' (1 Cor. 2:9)." Paul quoted verses from Isaiah 64:4 and 65:17. That sounds a lot like, "My ways higher than your ways, and My thoughts than your thoughts," does it not?

But look at how Paul wrapped this passage up: "But God has revealed them..." (1 Cor. 2:10). What has He revealed? Those things that God prepared for those who love Him. "God has revealed them to us," the verse continues. Uh oh! Now we have no excuse. You can't say, "God's ways are higher than mine and His thoughts are not my thoughts, so I really don't know what God would do in this situation." No! Paul just told you that "God has revealed them to *us*." He has revealed *to us* the things that He prepared *for* us. It gets even better: "But God has revealed them to us through His Spirit. For the Spirit searches all things, yes, the deep things of God" (1 Cor. 2:10). Not just some things—the Spirit searches *all* things, even the *deep* things of God. He has made it possible for us to know His will and His thoughts on *any* issue, through the Holy Spirit.

Let me add one last scripture that tops this whole argument off with a cherry. Paul wrote to Timothy: "All Scripture is given by inspiration of God, and is profitable for doctrine, for reproof, for correction, for instruction in righteousness, that the man of God may be complete, thoroughly equipped for every good work" (2 Tim. 3:16–17). Paul, one chapter earlier, had already explained to Timothy how to learn God's thoughts, ways, and His will in 2 Timothy 2:15: "Be diligent to present yourself approved to God, a worker who does not need to be ashamed, rightly dividing the word of truth." Other translations say "study to show yourself approved," rather than "be diligent to present yourself approved." You learn God's will through God's *Word*!

In fact, God goes out of His way to explain to us what rights we have as His children and heirs to His kingdom:

> Christ has redeemed us from the curse of the law, having become a curse for us; for it is written, Cursed is everyone who hangs on a tree: that upon the Gentiles might come the blessing of Abraham in Christ Jesus,

that we might receive the promise of the Spirit through faith.

—Galatians 3:13–14

BELIEVERS SHOULD RECEIVE THE BLESSING OF ABRAHAM

We believers are to receive the promise of the Spirit, and the blessing of Abraham is supposed to come upon us. Earlier we went over the blessing of Abraham from the book of Deuteronomy. As we read, the blessing was all physical and material, and we saw that, in fact, they all did indeed come on Abraham and his children. Now, through Christ Jesus, those blessings are *ours*. Remember, they included such things as being blessed in the city and in the field. Well, we don't have too many fields today—only about 2 percent of all Americans are farmers—but we have suburbs that are not in the city. So you can say that we should be blessed in the city and blessed in the suburbs.

For nearly fifty years, there has been a trend that urban historians call white flight, in which previous white residents of central cities have fled as more and more people of color began to settle in the inner cities. Deuteronomy, specifically, the blessing of Abraham, tells me that I shouldn't have to worry about where I live. I could be in downtown Baghdad, which, as of this writing, is a war zone, and still be blessed. The blessing of Abraham included healthy children. Your offspring should be physically well and well-adjusted. Abraham's blessing was to come upon your basket and your kneading bowl. Again, when that was written, most Jews lived in an agrarian and agricultural society in which they put their produce in baskets and they made bread and other staples of life in their kneading bowl. A way of stating that today would be, "Blessed shall be your computer stations, your drafting boards, your law offices, your design business—whatever you work at to provide your daily needs will be blessed."

Abraham's blessing in Deuteronomy included being blessed coming in and going out. So as a believer you should be blessed every time you climb in your car and every time you get in an airplane. I used to be terrified to fly. When I came into a knowledge of the Word of God, I realized that was nothing but a fear of death. The devil was saying to me every time I got in a plane, "This plane is going to crash." Then I learned about the blessing of Abraham, and I now know that when I'm on that plane, even if no one else is blessed, they are safe because the Bible says I'm blessed when I go out. We've seen many times that other people, even people who didn't have very much faith (or possibly didn't believe at all), were blessed and prospered by just being in close proximity to Abraham and Jacob and others who did have faith. In the New Testament, we read that Paul once was shipwrecked, but he told everyone with him not to worry because God said he would protect Paul and that the others would be safe because of that. (See Acts 27:22–24.) Well, that's wonderful for Paul, but we, too, under the new covenant have this blessing if we are aware of it and take advantage of it.

One of the most relevant blessings to our current study is Deuteronomy 28:8, where it is written, "The LORD will command the blessing on you in your storehouses and in all to which you set your hand." Then that is followed up in verse 11 with: "And the LORD will grant you plenty of goods, in the fruit of your body, in the increase of your livestock, and in the produce of your ground, in the land to which the LORD swore to your fathers to give you." When it says, "The LORD will command the blessing on you in your storehouses," how can that be translated as anything other than material prosperity? The word *storehouses* is plural, so in modern vernacular that verse would read, "The Lord will command the blessing on you in your bank accounts and investments."

BELIEVERS HAVE A NEW (BETTER) COVENANT

There is only one way you can possibly misunderstand this, and that is to somehow claim that the new covenant supercedes, *but is not as good as*, the old covenant. That's like saying, "The Lord will bless you with a new television and then give you a radio." Huh? It could be the greatest radio in the world, but it won't do what a television can do. A truly new, better television would have the radio built into it. If what Jesus left us is supposed to be better than what the Jews had, wouldn't you think it would at least include the blessings they had?

Think about the history of the telephone and you'll see this instantly. The first telephones were huge monstrosities, the size of a small suitcase. You had to talk to an operator, who connected the number for you, and the places you could call were few and far between because not many lines were put up. By the 1960s, we had telephone lines everywhere, and the phones had gotten to be the size of a small box. Nonetheless, you still had it connected by a line to a wall, and it still only let you do one thing—person-to-person communication. Then in the 1970s, we started to get the first mobile phones, so you could make a call from your car. But these were very large, cumbersome, and extremely expensive. Still, we had added mobility to phone service. You no longer needed an operator, except in special circumstances. By the early 1990s, cell phone technology had come along and gave us telephones the size of a wallet, or smaller. You never needed an operator, even to obtain a number, and the phones did a dozen things besides just connecting you with other people: they had internet connections, clocks, datebooks, address books, text messaging, and so on. By the mid-1990s, new photography features had been added so not only could you take a picture with a cell phone, but you could send it to someone else. You could get live streaming stock market quotations with the cell phone and play internet games. Now the newest generation of cell phone technology is including movie download capacity, so you can receive a movie or a television show on your cell phone via the Internet.

Imagine that you had a contract with, say, Bell Telephone for one of those box-sized phones of the 1960s. Here comes a "new covenant," a new contract with the phone company for phone service. And say they give you an address book and maybe a clock, but there is no phone service! What kind of new contract would that be? Who would want that? Even if the new service included Internet capability, you'd now have to go somewhere else to get the original "blessing" of the old phone service.

Do you see the point now? Jesus gave us a new covenant, which *begins* by giving us all the blessing of Abraham under the old covenant and *supercedes* that by giving us far more—spiritual blessings, including eternal life, sonship with the Almighty, the Holy Spirit, and so on. John wrote, "But as many as received Him, to them He gave the right to become children of God" (John 1:12). Have you received Jesus as your Savior and Lord? If so, you are a child of God. Only those people who have received Him as Savior and Lord are children of God. You can see this by inverting this verse with negatives: "But as many as did not receive Him, to them He did not give the right to become children of God." Abraham was a *servant* of God—he could not be a son of God because Jesus hadn't died and been resurrected yet, so Abe had no way into the family of God. He was a servant. Let me ask you a question: how many servants do you know who get preferential treatment over the children of the house? Not many, right? You have to have a pretty messed up family for a father to leave his butler or maid the inheritance instead of his son or daughter. Can we agree then that the children normally receive the inheritance?

What does this new will, or new covenant (inheritance), consist of? A full study of who we are in Christ and what we have in Christ would take another book. You can find dozens of descriptions of this in 2 Corinthians alone. I recommend that you read that book and look for any verse that begins with "You are" or "Don't you know you are" for the scriptural evidence of who you are in Christ.

We know that we have security and confidence that all the things we need will be provided. Look at Matthew 6:25, where Jesus said, "Therefore I say to you, do not worry about your life, what you will eat or what you will drink; nor about your body, what you will put on." Why, Jesus? How can we not worry? He gives us the answer in verse 33: "But seek first the kingdom of God and His righteousness, and all these things shall be added to you." In Matthew 7:7–8, He reiterates that promise: "Ask, and it will be given to you; seek, and you will find; knock and it will be opened to you. For everyone who asks receives, and he who seeks finds, and to him who knocks it will be opened."

Right away, some of you will say, "Wait a minute! Earlier you said, 'Give, and it will be given to you,' and now it's 'Ask, and it will be given to you.' Which is it? Isn't this a contradiction?" Not at all. As we will see later when we get to the actual process of prosperity, they are two separate steps. Go back to the businessman in chapter one: he leases space, obtains raw materials, hires a workforce, and makes the product. All this is part of "giving" in the economic sense. His product is ready. Now he takes orders, ships it off, and receives his first check. From that check, he tithes 10 percent. That's still part of the "giving," but this is the spiritual part, the obedience part. In between, he prays for God's blessing on his business venture. He *asks*, "Father, as You directed me, I founded this business and made this product. Now I ask your blessing, that you will sell everything we made." Both parts are necessary. Giving enables God to provide for you, but if you don't ask, you won't receive. Go back to Jesus' promise: "Ask, and it will be given to you; seek and you will find" (Matt. 7:7). The reverse of that must be true: "don't ask and it won't be given to you; and if you don't seek, you won't find."

Jesus also tells us, "For whoever does the will of My Father in heaven is My brother and sister and mother" (Matt. 12:50). Again, what did we see in chapter one? That God is wealthy beyond imagination. Jesus is His Son. We are Jesus' brothers and sisters. Does that not mean we are the sons and daughters of the richest Dad in the whole universe? Paul said in 1 Corinthians 1:4–7:

> I thank my God always concerning you for the grace of God which was given to you by Christ Jesus, that you were enriched in everything by Him in all utterance and all knowledge, even as the testimony of Christ was confirmed in you, so that you come short in no gift.

It seems pretty clear here that Jesus Christ enriched you in everything. How much is left out of "everything"? Would that enrichment not include both material and spiritual blessings? Then he repeated it: "so that you come short in *no* gift" (v. 7). How many gifts are left out then?

Is prosperity a gift? Are clothes gifts? Cars?

The language here is unmistakable, and you have to be dishonest to miss this: "enriched," "come short in no gift," "all these things will be added to you." Paul put it another way in Galatians 3:13: "Christ has redeemed us from the curse of the law, having become a curse for us." So we are to receive all the blessing of Abraham and none of the curse! Again, there is no doubt this refers to believers. Paul wrote in Galatians 3:16, "Now to Abraham and his Seed were the promises made. He does not say, 'And to seeds,' as of many, but as of one, 'And to your Seed,' who is Christ." By pinning this down to Jesus Christ, Paul made it impossible for people to argue that these blessings now were supposed to befall all mankind. You frequently hear the phrase, the "fatherhood of God and the brotherhood of man." Well, the blessing only works if you are indeed born of God. You are not my brother or sister unless we have the same Father—Jehovah God. A Buddhist is not my brother because he doesn't have the same Father as I have. That doesn't mean I can mistreat him, and that doesn't exempt me from loving him and praying for his salvation. However, it does mean that as of right now he does not have the same rights as I do or as other members of my "family" do, because he ain't in the family.

Only the Seed of Abraham, Jesus, is entitled to the covenant promises. Since we belong to Jesus—in fact we are His body—we are entitled to those promises too. "And let us not grow weary while doing good," Paul continues, "for in due

99

season we shall reap if we do not lose heart" (Gal. 6:9). Again, Paul reiterated in Ephesians 3:3 that God "made known to me the mystery" which he went on to say "in other ages was not made known to the sons of men, as it has now been revealed by the Spirit to His holy apostles and prophets: that the Gentiles should be fellow heirs, of the same body, and partakers of His promise in Christ through the gospel" (Eph. 3:5–6). We are the seed of Abraham through Jesus, fellow heirs, and of the same body as Jesus, and because of that we are also "partakers of His [God's] promise in Christ."

Some of the other promises to which Christians may lay claim were guaranteed us by the life, death, and resurrection of Christ. Consider the Psalm 23:1–6:

> The LORD is my shepherd; I shall not want. He makes me to lie down in green pastures; He leads me beside the still waters. He restores my soul; He leads me in the paths of righteousness For His name's sake. Yea, though I walk through the valley of the shadow of death, I will fear no evil; for You are with me; Your rod and Your staff, they comfort me. You prepare a table before me in the presence of my enemies; You anoint my head with oil; My cup runs over. Surely goodness and mercy shall follow me All the days of my life; and I will dwell in the house of the LORD Forever.

You say, "That's the old covenant. How do you know that is for Christians, too?" Jesus said in John 10:14, "I am the good shepherd; and I know My sheep, and am known by My own." For the Twenty-third Psalm to apply to you, you have to be one of His sheep. And you cannot be one of His sheep unless you have been born again.

Let's examine this Twenty-third Psalm and see some of the blessings it promises to believers.

First, after stating that "The Lord is my shepherd"—and not just *a* shepherd—the psalmist says, "I shall not want" (v. 1). We know millions of Christians, however, are in want. Early in my faith walk, at the very time in my life that I was quoting the Twenty-third Psalm, the power company was shutting off my lights because I couldn't pay the bill. I was in want. You can be a Christian and still be in a situation of need if you do not know God's promises and how to put them into action. I just talked about the power company. In every room in your house there is a light switch. The power company is shooting energy through those lines twenty-four hours a day, nonstop. But you can sit in the dark and eat cold food unless you turn on the lights and the microwave. It's up to you. The power company did its part. So you can't blame the power company for not having light if you didn't turn the switch on. Every day, however, people blame God for not providing for them when they sit there with the switches turned off.

The psalmist says God "leads me beside the still waters" (v. 2). When the waters are quiet, you can wade in them without fear of being inundated by the flood. "He restores my soul," which is a reference to salvation (v. 3). When you were born again, you experienced a spiritual rebirth. As Paul wrote in 2 Corinthians 5:17, "Therefore, if anyone is in Christ, he is a new creation." The psalmist also says, "Yea, though I walk through the valley of the shadow of death, I will fear no evil" (v. 4). It does not say, "Yea, though I walk through the valley of death." Death has no rightful claim on His sheep, so only the *shadow* of the valley of death can come upon us. Years ago I went to a zoo. As we were passing some of the cages, I saw my shadow and a form was moving over it. When I looked up, there was a cage with a huge boa constrictor. That snake couldn't hurt me—the only thing that snake was touching was my shadow. I don't have to fear evil. I don't even have to fear death, because Jesus has given us victory over death, too. "O death, where is your sting? O Hades, where is your victory?" asks Paul in 1 Corinthians 15:55, after Jesus defeated hell and death. We, in Him, have victory over both.

The psalmist says, "You prepare a table before me in the presence of my enemies; You anoint my head with oil; My cup runs over." It doesn't matter who your enemies are, whether they are business rivals or people trying to steal your inventions. God has promised His children that He would prepare a table for us right under the noses of our enemies. The success will be so amazing that those who wished you ill are going to have to sit in amazement as you reap blessings in front of them. Don't get upset if your enemies appear to get the upper hand for a season. Stay obedient and stay in faith. Soon, you will be able to say with complete assurance, "You anoint my head with oil; my cup runs over" (Ps. 23:5). In Jesus' day, only royalty routinely had their heads anointed with oil. You will get to the point you can say, "Too much! My cup is running over. Where else can I invest in the kingdom of God?"

It's rare, but there are people who go to bed every night saying to themselves, "What am I going to do with all this money?" There is nothing else they want and nothing really for them to buy. That's an overflowing cup. For a believer, there is never a point at which you say, "What am I going to do with all this money?" because, at least in the near future, there are a million things that need money in order to advance the kingdom. There are always more hospitals to build, more missions to establish, more teachers to train, and so on. As we will see in our final sections, it is the selfish person who says, "Oh, I have enough. I don't need anymore." Well, maybe *you* don't need anymore, but what about the struggling minister in Indonesia who must battle the Muslim clerics every day? Or the doctor in Zimbabwe who has a hospital full of AIDS patients? Stop thinking about yourself! One purpose of prosperity is that you are blessed and have more than enough, but your cup runs over so that you will give that spillover to someone in need!

All of this was established in the blessing of Abraham. Jesus, however, died and rose from the grave to give us an even better covenant. Hebrews 8:6 says, "But now He has obtained a more excellent ministry, inasmuch as He is also Mediator of a better covenant, which was established on better promises." Because Jesus was perfect and "offered Himself without spot to God" (Heb. 9:14), He is, as Paul said, "...the Mediator of the new covenant, by means of death, for the redemption of the transgressions under the first covenant, that those who are called may receive the promise of eternal inheritance" (Heb. 9:15).

OTHER BLESSINGS OF THE NEW COVENANT

What are the additional, new conditions of this new covenant? Hebrews 9:28 says, "So Christ was offered once to bear the sins of many. To those who eagerly wait for Him He will appear a second time, apart from sin, for salvation." One thing that better covenant gives us is eternal life, thanks to Christ who "was offered once to bear the sins of many." Because of His sacrifice, Paul then explains that we can come before God without a human priest: "Therefore, brethren, having boldness to enter the Holiest by the blood of Jesus" (Heb. 10:19). We now have the authority to come directly before God. If you remember, only Moses could speak with God, then, later, only the Levitical High Priest after extensive ceremonial preparation.

What does this have to do with finances? Plenty! It means that now you can take your financial appeals directly to God. Philippians 4:6 tells us, "Be anxious for nothing, but in everything by prayer and supplication, with thanksgiving, let your requests be made known to God." OK, then what, Paul? "And my God shall supply all your need according to His riches in glory by Christ Jesus" (Phil. 4:19). Thanks to the new covenant, not only do we have a right to the blessing of Abraham, all of the blessings of the psalmist, but now anything that wasn't directly covered in those promises we can take to God directly—with "prayer and supplication, with thanksgiving" and God will supply all your need. There is not one thing you have a right to be anxious for, then. There is not one thing that you can need that God will not supply you.

Remember, a covenant is an agreement—a contract—and like any contract, there are conditions. Attorneys call these "conditions of performance." For you to get paid, you must do something. For a certain clause to be null and void, someone must fail to do something. If you have a warranty on a new car, for example, but never take it in to have it serviced, that will void your warranty. It's not the company's fault: Ford or Toyota or whoever was willing to fix anything that broke during a certain period of time, but to ensure that it did not break in the first place, you had to keep the car well-oiled, the radiator full, and so on.

Our new covenant, which is a better, more extensive contract with Almighty God, has conditions. We will see in a later chapter exactly what those conditions are and how you can void your contract with God if you don't perform. Of course, we have an enemy, and the enemy has had control of the world's system of finances since Adam's sin. God can bless and protect us within that system, but living outside of God's covenant, you are on your own in terms of surviving the system. In the next chapter, we'll turn our attention to the world's view of prosperity and how the vast majority of the people will never have a chance of getting ahead in such a system.

Notes

Notes

Chapter 5
THE WORLD'S PROSPERITY SYSTEM

A COMMON MISCONCEPTION IS that our heavenly Father is the ruler of this world. God is the Creator of the heavens and the earth, but He gave dominion—right or authority—over to Adam long ago, and Adam transferred those rights to Satan when he sinned against God back in the garden. Jesus said at the judgment, "The ruler of this world will be cast out" (John 12:31). So if the devil hasn't been cast out yet, he is still the ruler of this world. Jesus said in John 10:10, referring to the devil, "The thief does not come except to steal, and to kill, and to destroy."

Satan does not intend any good to come to any person. He will, however, bring riches into the hands of certain people *temporarily* to make it appear that serving him is profitable. Even if those he brings wealth to are not demonstrably on his side, the very fact that they are not born again and that they cannot call Jehovah their Father makes them the devil's children. Jesus, always one to speak plainly, said to the Pharisees in John 8:44, "You are of your father the devil." People today shun such blunt talk, but the Lord said to these religious men, in essence, "You guys are the sons of Satan!" Paul was saying, "You were already dead!" in Colossians 2:13, when he began, "And you, being dead in your trespasses..." Without Jesus, we are already spiritually dead.

You might see wealthy, successful people who are not Christians but who are "good" by the world's standards:

They give generously to various civic and charitable causes. There are hospital wings and libraries named after them. Hundreds of students attend colleges on scholarships they provided. Remember, though, that the world judges people by their works, not by their confession of Jesus Christ as their Savior. What did Paul say about those who were without Christ? "Therefore remember that you, once Gentiles in the flesh....were without Christ, being aliens from the common-wealth of Israel and strangers from the covenants of promise, having no hope and without God in the world" (Eph. 2:11–12). Jesus said in Mark 8:38, "For whoever is ashamed of Me and My words in this adulterous and sinful generation, of him the Son of Man will also be ashamed when He comes in the glory of His Father with the holy angels." Again, He said in Luke 11:23, "He who is not with Me is against Me, and he who does not gather with Me scatters." And He said in Luke 12:9: "But he who denies Me before men will be denied before the angels of God."

The point is, there are no "goodie points" with God for giving away money, or for doing good works. There is only one way to God: "If you confess with your mouth the Lord Jesus and believe in your heart that God has raised Him from the dead, you will be saved" (Rom. 10:9). Paul wrote in Ephesians 2:1: "And you He made alive, who were dead in trespasses and sins." Merely good people, no matter how good they are, are already spiritually dead! Have you ever gone camping and put pieces of paper into a fire? The fire doesn't care if it's burning up a comic book or Shakespeare. Both are consumed equally. It's irrelevant what was written on the paper—how "good" it was. It was still paper, turned to ashes by flames. What was on them was not relevant to what they both were, namely pieces of paper. Those who are good people in the world's eyes, even those rich people who generously give away money, are in God's eyes no different than the mobsters who do not give away their riches. It's not about the money—it's about Jesus!

So what, exactly, is the world system of getting wealth, and how does it work with a spirit of poverty? In 1 Timothy 6:17 Paul wrote, "Command those [believers] who are rich in this present age not to be haughty, nor to trust in uncertain riches but in the living God, who gives us richly all things to enjoy." One fellow quipped that the world's system is to "get all you can, can all you get, and sit on your can!" That's not too far from the truth in today's world. Non-believers *trust* in riches. God did not tell Christians not to have riches, but not to "trust" in "uncertain riches."

WORLDLY WEALTH IS UNCERTAIN

All of the world's wealth is uncertain. Robert Morris, probably the wealthiest man in America in the 1780s, lost everything in less than a year when he tried to sell short his securities. He ended up in a debtor's prison. William "Billy" Durant, the founder of General Motors, lost everything he had in the Great Crash and finished his life operating a bowling alley. In the early 1990s, Rapper MC Hammer, now a minister of the gospel, squandered a fortune of twenty million dollars, pouring twelve million dollars into his house, which included a thirty-three-seat theater, two swimming pools, and a seventeen-car garage. Perhaps the most astounding "riches to rags" story is that of Samuel Insull. In 1929, Insull had a utility company empire worth $270 million (worth easily fifteen to twenty billion dollars today) just before the Crash, but was utterly bankrupt a year later. Think of that: $270 *million!* I know some of you say, "I'd never lose that amount of money!"[1] Oh really?

A study by the Certified Financial Planner Board found that nearly one-third of all lottery winners became bankrupt.[2] The *San Francisco Chronicle* reported the story of one Englishman who drank himself to death just two years after winning 1.8 million pounds ($2.57 million) in the lottery. The state of Virginia's lottery officials reported that in 1999, out of three hundred winners of at least a million dollars, sixty encountered financial problems within three years.[3] Stephen Goldbart, a psychologist in Great Britain who headed the Money, Meaning and Choices Institute found "a significant number of lottery winners lose their winnings within five years."[4]

Nor did these "uncertain" riches bring happiness. Another study found that after an initial euphoria, winning the lottery had no effect on a person's level of happiness.[5] In fact, a study conducted by American psychologists found that sudden, sharp increases in wealth for people unaccustomed to a lot of money actually caused unhappiness.[6] As we will see later, it is not the money that itself is the cause of happiness or unhappiness, but the *trust* people put in "uncertain" riches. Emory University researchers determined that "lottery winners, trust fund recipients, and others who get their money without working for it do not get nearly as much satisfaction from their cash as those who earn it the old fashioned way—by working at a regular job."[7] Kennon Sheldon, a psychologist at the University of Missouri at Columbia, stated, "We consistently find that people who say money is most important to them are [the unhappiest]."[8] It is common sense. Most of those who work regular jobs and who have built successful businesses appreciate how difficult it is to acquire wealth and how rapidly it can leave.

In Mark 4:14–19, Jesus explained the parable of the sower that He told in the verses just prior to that:

> The sower sows the word. And these are the ones by the wayside where the word is sown. When they hear, Satan comes immediately and takes away the word that was sown in their hearts. These likewise are the ones sown on stony ground who, when they hear the word, immediately receive it with gladness; and they have no root in themselves, and so endure only for a time. Afterward, when tribulation or persecution arises for the word's sake, immediately they stumble. Now these are the ones sown among thorns; they are the ones who hear the word, and the cares of this world, the deceitfulness of riches, and the desires for other things entering in choke the word, and it becomes unfruitful.

Jesus carefully differentiated between the "deceitfulness of riches" and riches; and between the "desires for other things" and the other things themselves.

As people acquire wealth, they tend to think they are invincible. If you think about it, money can buy many things in this world. It can't buy you love (as the Beatles used to sing), but it can sure buy you a companion for a night who will pretend to love you. In fact, wealthy men have their mistresses, most of whom pretend on a daily basis to love the man who supports them. Money can't buy you immortality, but you have to admit that, even in America, rich people can afford the best treatment and can even pull strings to get experimental drugs before other people. If you are so inclined, money can even get rid of your enemies for you.

All of this power, and all the things you think money can buy, is an illusion. It deceives. Look at the parable Jesus told in Luke 12:16–21:

> The ground of a certain rich man yielded plentifully. And he thought within himself, saying, "What shall I do, since I have no room to store my crops?" So he said, "I will do this: I will pull down my barns and build greater, and there I will store all my crops and my goods. And I will say to my soul, 'Soul, you have many goods laid up for many years; take your ease; eat, drink, and be merry.'" But God said to him, "Fool! This night your soul will be required of you; then whose will those things be which you have provided?" So is he who lays up treasure for himself, and is not rich toward God.

Jesus commanded us in Matthew 6:19–20, "Do not lay up for yourselves treasures on earth, where moth and rust destroy and where thieves break in and steal; but lay up for yourselves treasures in heaven, where neither moth nor rush destroys and where thieves do not break in and steal." It's interesting that He used that phrase, "where thieves do not break in and steal," because as we saw in John 10:10 He said, "The thief does not come except to steal, and to kill, and to destroy."

Whatever treasures you lay up in heaven are immune to the world's system. Satan—the thief—cannot touch them. That's why you cannot focus on earthly wealth, but on heavenly riches. Paul put it this way in 1 Timothy 6:19: "Storing up for themselves a good foundation for the time to come, that they may lay hold on eternal life." The world's system focuses on the material and the physical. It tells you there is no God, and there is only what you make out of life. God's prosperity system requires that you start with the spiritual, and it will eventually be revealed in this material world.

FAITH VS. FEAR

The difference between the two systems—God's system of prosperity and the devil's world system—is summed up in two words: *faith* and *fear.* We will see later that God's plan is based entirely on faith. The world's system is based on fear. All money issues are, essentially, fear issues. You might ask, "Isn't it about greed?" Actually, almost all greed is really rooted in fear. Why does a millionaire chase that next dollar? Down deep, he is afraid he will lose that money he already possesses. Greed, or the lust for money, is a control issue. People think that more money will allow them to control their lives, making life risk free. You and I know that life is never risk free in terms of the devil shooting darts at you. Paul even said that the fiery darts of the wicked one would come, but if you have on your shield of faith, they will be quenched. God never removes temptations, trials, and tests, but rather gives you the way of escape. Paul wrote, "No temptation has overtaken you except such as is common to man; but God is faithful, who will not allow you to be tempted beyond what you are able, but with the temptation will also make the way of escape, that you may be able to bear it" (1 Cor. 10:13).

Greed is a variation on fear. It is fear of want—fear of lack. Again, people think that within their own power they can build up enough wealth that nothing can harm them. You cannot be secure in life, no matter how much money you have, if you live each day in fear. Some of God's greatest men and women have developed huge chinks in their armor when it came to fear, and it cost them. Consider Job. How many of you have ever said, "The Lord giveth and the Lord taketh away"? (See Job 1:21.) Perhaps many of you sincerely believe that this is a statement of truth taken from the Bible. However, while everything in the Bible is truly stated (i.e., quoted correctly), everything that was recorded in the Bible is not a statement of truth.

Let me give you a modern example. Say I am the chairman of the board of General Motors, and at the annual meeting, where we have a secretary taking down the minutes of the meeting, I bang the gavel and say, "The Nineteenth Annual Meeting of the Stockholders of General Motors will come to order." The secretary writes that down. But there's a problem—I meant the ninetieth annual meeting, not the nineteenth. Usually, in a public forum, people will just let that gaffe pass and will amend it in the minutes later on. But I said it—it's recorded right there in the minutes. It's just not accurate. It is not a statement of truth.

So we have Job as an example. In chapter 1 of the book of Job, we find that Satan approaches the throne of God and asks permission to attack His servant, Job. God grants Satan permission. Realize, God did not give Satan authority he didn't already have. However, as long as Job stayed within God's plan, and as long as Job stayed in faith, the devil couldn't touch him. Yet we see in verses 12–19 that Job's servants were killed and herds stolen, then his children were all killed. Job responded in this famous line, "...Naked I came from my mother's womb, And naked shall I return there. The LORD gave, and the LORD has taken away; Blessed be the name of the LORD." That line has even been made into a key lyric of a very popular contemporary Christian song, "Blessed Be Your Name," by a group called Tree 63.

There is one small problem.

God didn't take anything away. The devil came out the big winner in that exchange because not only did he get to destroy Job's wealth and kill his children, but he managed to get God blamed for it! For centuries, churches have been quoting that line as though "thus saith the Lord." But what really happened in this episode?

We find in Job 1:1 that Job himself was "blameless and upright, and one who feared God and shunned evil." Right there is the reason God can later say to the devil, "Behold, all that he has is in your power; only do not lay a hand on his person" (Job 1:12). God could say that because Job had not given the devil an opening into his *personal life* through his thoughts, actions, or behavior. But Job was not perfect. He had a weakness: For the thing I greatly feared has come upon me, And what I dreaded has happened to me" (Job 3:25). Job was a man afraid. He was not walking in complete faith. Obviously he did not fear death, because the devil couldn't kill him. What was he afraid of? "For Job said, 'It may be that my sons have sinned and cursed God in their hearts'" (Job 1:5). Job was afraid that his sons (and daughters) were sinning. We have to infer from what is actually said in scripture at this point, but we see in Job 1:18 that a messenger came to Job and said, "Your sons and daughters were eating and drinking wine in their oldest brother's house" when the house fell in on them and killed them. So it looks as though Jobs' children were, in our modern vernacular, party animals. Otherwise, why would Job be concerned that they had cursed God in their hearts? I never once was worried that any of my three daughters or my son had cursed God in their hearts. Job knew something was up with his kids, and he feared the consequences for them.

Later, Job says in 19:6, "Know then that God has wronged me, and has surrounded me with His net." Yet Psalm 91:3 says, "He shall deliver you from the snare of the fowler," not throw you in the net! In Job 12:9, he asks, "Who among all these does not know that the hand of the LORD has done this?" But God did not do it—the devil did. Although Job stands firm, he doesn't do so without extensive complaining and pig-headed stubbornness. He says in Job 7:11, "I will speak in the anguish of my spirit; I will complain in the bitterness of my soul," and repeats, "I will speak in the bitterness of my soul" in verse 10:1, which indicates he is willfully speaking evil, rather than faith. Job eventually came around, and God gave him an out through obedience. But I wanted to show you that this was *Job's opinion* of why those things happened to him, and *not what actually occurred!* Moreover, I wanted you to see that this all started with Job's fear, and when he got into fear, he was no longer in faith.

Greed is a form of fear. One millionaire—the quotation is often ascribed to John D. Rockefeller—was asked how much is enough, and he reportedly answered "one dollar more." Why would one dollar more make a difference? It would only make a difference if you were insecure or afraid. What was Jesus' response to the same question?

> Therefore I say to you, do not worry about your life, what you will eat or what you will drink; nor about your body, what you will put on. Is not life more than food and the body more than clothing? Look at the birds of the air, for they neither sow nor reap nor gather into barns; yet your heavenly Father feeds them. Are you not of more value than they? Which of you by worrying can add one cubit to his stature? So why do you worry about clothing? Consider the lilies of the

field, how they grow: they neither toil nor spin; and yet I say to you that even Solomon in all his glory was not arrayed like one of these. Now if God so clothes the grass of the field, which today is, and tomorrow is thrown into the oven, will He not much more clothe you, O you of little faith? Therefore do not worry, saying, "What shall we eat?" or "What shall we drink?" or "What shall we wear?" For after all these things the Gentiles seek. For your heavenly Father knows that you need all these things. But seek first the kingdom of God and His righteousness, and all these things shall be added to you.

—Matthew 6:25–33

Worry is just another variation on fear, and from verses 25 to 34 Jesus used the phrase "do not worry" or "why do you worry" four times. We could just as easily say, do not be afraid, or, why are you afraid? because He was addressing the fear of lack. The greedy think that having more will protect them against the lack they fear. But the problem isn't lack. Rather, the problem is fear. In 2 Timothy 1:7, Paul wrote to Timothy, "For God has not given us a spirit of fear, but of power and of love and of a sound mind." Fear is not from God. Fear is from the devil.

There was a time when my fears had fears. I was afraid of flying. I was afraid of water—something that stemmed from my childhood when I was dropped under the surface of the ocean. It got to the point where I couldn't stand to even put my face into the water in the shower. Once I learned the Word, however, that was the end of Mr. Fear. Once I found out that God had not given me a spirit of fear, I stopped accepting fear. Today, I love to swim and scuba dive, and while flying is rarely "fun" unless you are a pilot; it sure beats driving by car across country for hours on end. I no longer have the slightest fear about climbing into an airplane.

Matthew 14:22–32 gives the account of Jesus walking on water, and provides us with a clear example of fear at work. From inside the boat, Peter saw Jesus walking toward him on the water and said, "Lord, if it is You, command me to come to You on the water" (v. 28). Jesus told him to come, and Peter began to walk on water. "But when [Peter] saw that the wind was boisterous, he was afraid; and beginning to sink he cried out, saying, 'Lord, save me!'" He grew fearful. Your senses will feed you fear. When you open the mail and see those bills, it will shake your faith in God's ability to provide! They are right there in front of you, and your mind starts to go wild. What if I can't pay these? What if they repossess my car? What if I'm made homeless? You find yourself beginning to sink. The devil knows how to use fear on your finances.

Greed that is born out of fear is only another variation on the theme. Paul confirmed how fear and greed are related. In Hebrews 13:5–6, he wrote, "Let your conduct be without covetousness; be content with such things as you have. For He Himself has said, 'I will never leave you nor forsake you.' So we may boldly say: 'The LORD is my helper; I will not fear. What can man do to me?'" Why should you not covet? Why should you be content with what you have? *Because the Lord can always supply more.* You don't need to want what someone else has—stop just wanting it and ask for it! Look also at this: "I will not fear" sounds a lot like the Twenty-third Psalm, which says, "I shall not want" (v. 1). Want and fear are fellow travelers, mirror images of the same spiritual issue—control.

Look at the similar phrase in each: "I will not/I shall not." In each case, it is a *choice* as to what you do. Being afraid is a choice. Being in want is a choice. Being content is a choice. Paul wrote to the church at Philippi, "I have learned in whatever state I am, to be content" (Phil. 4:11). He said he had *learned* to be content. Paul continued, "I know how to be abased, and I know how to abound. Everywhere and in all things I have learned both to be full and to be hungry, both to abound and to suffer need" (v. 12). Paul said he knew *how* to do it. It didn't say that being abased was better than abounding.

If you are a Christ-follower, you should abound in every area of your life. That is what the Word of God says. So you would have to learn to suffer need; that is, you would have to learn to make yourselves hungry. God doesn't want you lazy: He wants you in need, insofar as you need Him! You need to learn to abound in Him and to understand your need in Him. There is an old Rocky movie where his former opponent and now trainer, Apollo Creed, tells Rocky Balboa that he had gotten too comfortable and too soft. He no longer had the "eye of the tiger."[8] Staying hungry, staying full of that same level of intensity you had when you thought you needed God for everything is actually hard to do when all your needs are met. That's why you must *learn* it. It is a discipline.

From everything we know about Paul, he is likely the most disciplined Christian in human history. He spent years bringing himself under control so that he could then say in Philippians 4:13, "I can do all things through Christ who strengthens me." This same Paul said, "Be anxious for nothing, but in everything by prayer and supplication, with thanksgiving, let your requests be made known to God" (Phil. 4:6). Paul could "do all things" because he was anxious for nothing.

THE RICH YOUNG RULER

One of the most famous money episodes in the Bible is in Matthew 19:16–22. Look at these verses in the context of fear:

> Now behold, one came and said to Him, "Good Teacher, what good thing shall I do that I may have eternal life?" So He said to him, "Why do you call Me good? No one is good but One, that is, God. But if you want to enter into life, keep the commandments." He said to Him, "Which ones?" Jesus said, "'You shall not murder,' 'You shall not commit adultery,' 'You shall not steal,' 'You shall not bear false witness,' 'Honor your father and your mother,' and, 'You shall love your neighbor as yourself.'" The young man said to Him, "All these things I have kept from my youth. What do I still lack?" Jesus said to him, "If you want to be perfect, go, sell what you have and give to the poor, and you will have treasure in heaven; and come, follow Me." But when the young man heard that saying, he went away sorrowful, for he had great possessions.

We don't know for sure, but the implication is that this young man knew Jesus and had been following Him for some time. He certainly knew Jesus was good and that He had been teaching on eternal life. Mark's description of this incident in Mark 10:17–22 says the man came "running." That was highly unusual, because in Jewish culture, it was unseemly for men to run except into battle. Mark also says he "knelt before Him" (v. 17). He was willing to humble himself, willing to kneel, and yet when the issue came to his wealth, "he went away sorrowful" (v. 22).

Why did this rich young man go away? Because of fear. He was afraid that if he gave away his great possessions he would never get them back. Notice even the very wording that this man used in Matthew 19:20: "What do I still *lack*?" This rich man—he's often called the "rich young ruler," but in Matthew there is no reference to him being any kind of ruler—was living in a poverty mind-set. He was obsessed with lack. His fear was that he would loose his great possessions.

While this verse is quoted correctly, I think the meaning is often misunderstood when it says, "For he had great possessions." I think what is actually meant there is, "For great possessions had him!" The things controlled him. He couldn't give them up. Notice what Jesus did *not* say: He did not say, "Sell what you have and give *all of it* to the poor." I believe that the Lord was not interested in what this man gave, but rather in his willingness to give. Jesus did not command him to give everything away. He wanted to see obedience—a trend. Personally, I think that if this young man had sold what he had and demonstrated his commitment to follow Jesus by beginning to give, the Lord would have said, "That's enough. Leverage your wealth for the kingdom now!" But the riches had him, and he couldn't give them up, not even when someone he respected as a Good Teacher promised him he would have treasure in heaven.

Fear and its twin-image, greed, govern the world's system. A Christian has no business being in fear. One of the most often-used phrases in the New Testament, by both Jesus and the angels, is "Fear not!" You cannot simultaneously be in fear and in faith. One of the cornerstone verses of my ministry has always been 2 Corinthians 5:7: "For we walk by faith, not by sight." In Hebrews 11:6, Paul wrote "But without faith it is impossible to please Him, for he who comes to God must believe that He is, and that He is a rewarder of those who diligently seek Him."

Ask people who have been married for some time what their greatest challenges were. Most of them will not say sexual problems, but rather financial problems. Marriages are never under greater stress than when the finances are bad. Why? Because it calls into question the whole issue of trust, especially if the man is the main breadwinner. When he can't pay the bills, the wife wonders, "Can I trust him, not only to keep me safe and to pay for our house, but to care for our children?" That trust issue is a fear issue. Her real concern is based on fear that he will not be able to support her and their children. The last thing the devil wants is for you to cast aside your fears—to fear not!—and rely on God.

Early in my marriage, I came to one of those points when I just wasn't making enough money to pay the bills. Naturally, it started an argument. I tried to defend myself by saying, "I'm doing the best I can!" Betty responded, "Well that's just not good enough!" Man, talk about a shot through the heart. But she was right. It wasn't good enough, because I was relying on my weak old self, not on God. Once I learned the Word, she's never again had to tell me that my best wasn't good enough.

Over the centuries, the devil has distorted all teachings on money every which way he could to keep Christians from letting God prosper them. Think about it: if he can keep Christians in a poverty mentality and keep money out of their hands, his job is much easier. He doesn't have to worry about thousands of Bibles being translated and circulated in remote parts of the world; he doesn't have to worry about television signals beaming off satellites. All these things cost money.

SATAN'S STRATEGY

Satan's main lines of attack have been twofold. First, he has persuaded some Christians that no action at all is needed on their part to acquire wealth. Second—his favorite tactic—has been to try to convince Christians that money is bad and that being wealthy is sinful. The first of these tactics involved the doctrine of predestination, which essentially held that "whoever is saved is already saved, and whoever is damned is already damned" and there isn't anything you can do to change your pre-ordained situation. Technically, of course, predestination requires that the person make a confession of faith, but, for all intents and purposes, God already determined that the person would do that anyway. Predestination became an economic issue in the 1500s when groups of Calvinists, and later the English Puritans, came to believe that one way to demonstrate that you were saved was by being blessed in this world, since God would bless whom He had already saved. That led them to work hard, save, and invest. Because the natural law of sowing and reaping was being utilized, they ultimately received profits of these practices. Many of the Puritans, in particular, grew quite wealthy.

But another subgroup took the opposite view, and this has trickled down to us even to the present. Their view was that whoever God wants to bless, He'll bless; and whoever He doesn't want to bless, He won't. There is nothing we can do about it. We have no role in our own prosperity. What does the Bible say about that? Deuteronomy 8:18 says, "And you shall remember the LORD your God, for it is He who gives you power to get wealth." Notice the verse did not say that God "gives you wealth." No, it says God "gives *you* the *power* to get wealth." The responsibility is yours to get the wealth. God makes it possible for you to get it, but you must take action! Some people will read Philippians 4:19—"And my God shall supply all your need according to His riches in glory by Christ Jesus"—and think, "Well, God will supply it so I don't need to work!" Surely you know better.

In 2 Thessalonians 3:10, Paul wrote "For even when we were with you, we commanded you this: If anyone will not work, neither shall he eat." Again, Paul wrote to Timothy, "But if anyone does not provide for his own, and especially for those of his household, he has denied the faith and is worse than an unbeliever" (1 Tim. 5:8). You don't get much clearer than that. Christians are to work and are expected to *at the very least* provide for their own households. Jesus worked as a carpenter, which is not what we in America consider a cushy job. Paul was a tentmaker and continued to work even after he became an apostle. (See Acts 20:34.)

While some Christians are challenged by the requirement to work, it is not nearly as serious a problem in the church as the second way that the devil tries to derail prosperity, and that is through demonizing money and wealth. We need a little history lesson here.

Over the course of two thousand years, Satan has been quite successful at persuading many Christians that God wants them poor. This got its start in medieval times when the Roman Catholic Church worked out arrangements with various monarchs in which the church would have the final word in spiritual matters (defining heresy, blasphemy, and so on) while the king maintained complete authority when it came to politics (areas such as treason). There was even a time that when kings were crowned, a bishop or priest would put the crown on his head. This action symbolized to the people that God had put that ruler on the throne and that his authority was by "divine right"—which of course was often not the case. In exchange for receiving freedom to control spiritual issues, the church had to help the rulers keep the peasants in line. One of the best ways to do that was to remind the peasants that, because of their poverty—often equated with humility—God loved them more than He loved the nobles. Peasants could feel a little better that the rich folk would get theirs on the other side, while they, the poor, would have eternal rewards.

None of this came from the Bible, yet it was passed down for hundreds of years in the Roman Catholic Church and then, after the Protestant Reformation, through several denominations of Protestant churches. Some Bible verses were taken out of context, as we saw with Job 1:21 ("The LORD gave, and the LORD has taken away"); many were consistently misinterpreted to paint wealth or money in a bad light. Take 1 Timothy 6:10, for example:

> For the love of money is a root of all kinds of evil, for which some have strayed from the faith in their greediness, and pierced themselves through with many sorrows.

Perhaps no other verse in the Bible is as misquoted as this one. It does not say, "For money is the root of all evil, for which some have strayed from the faith." Money is not evil. Almost anything on earth can be used for good or evil. It's hard to think of anything that is evil in and of itself. Moldy bread will make you vomit—but that same mold can produce penicillin. Poppy seeds can make heroin, which can turn people into junkies, but that same opiate can help alleviate pain when you have a severe injury. A little aspirin will help with a headache, but if you take the whole bottle, it will burn a hole in your stomach. Money has no inherent morality. Paul said the problem was the *love* of money, then he further qualified that as a root of "all kinds of evil." Not *all* evil. There's plenty of evil that comes from things other than money.

Some of the greediest people on earth are the poorest. You don't have to have a million dollars to be greedy. You can love money and not have a dime of it. The street-corner mugger is no different than the corporate embezzler in his intent. They both love money so much they want someone else's, as well as their own. Yet over the centuries, when this verse was read or discussed, do you think these distinctions were made very often? I doubt it. That's why so many people to this day still misquote this verse.

Sometimes you can quote one part of the Bible correctly, but if you don't put it in the context of another part, you can get entirely the wrong meaning. Here is another often-misquoted verse: "Blessed are the poor." How many times have you heard that? Luke indeed wrote, "Then He lifted up His eyes toward His disciples, and said: 'Blessed are you poor, For yours is the kingdom of God" (Luke 6:20). We will return to Luke's version of this, but look at how Matthew put it: "Blessed are the poor *in spirit*, for theirs is the kingdom of heaven" (Matt. 5:3, emphasis added). So He wasn't talking about earthly riches or earthly poverty here—it's clear the contrast is between the poor *in spirit* and the rich *in spirit*. If you go back to our earlier discussion of why people prior to Jesus' resurrection could only be blessed in material/physical things, this makes sense. They were poor in spirit because they were spiritually dead! Jesus now made them abundant in spiritual things—or soon would, after the resurrection.

Luke went on in his Gospel to quote Jesus saying: "But woe to you who are rich, For you have received your consolation"

(Luke 6:24). Did this mean He condemned earthly riches? Look at the following verses, if you think so: "Woe to you who are full, For you shall hunger. Woe to you who laugh now, For you shall mourn and weep" (Luke 6:25). If you use the logic that He was addressing earthly riches, then you have to say that it is forbidden to laugh or to eat enough to be full. Yet we know Jesus constantly instructed us (for example, in Luke 6:23) to rejoice. You cannot rejoice and at the same time be in mourning. It's impossible. The middle of the word *rejoice* is *joy*, and joy implies laughter. Show me a joyful mourner. It's an oxymoron, like a jumbo shrimp or a meat-less cow. No, in the Luke passages, Jesus was saying that you will reap woe if you choose earthly material things over Him. In earlier chapters I explained that we must keep His kingdom first, and all things we need on this earth will follow.

Yet century after century, poverty was held up as virtuous, while the acquisition of wealth was viewed as ungodly. It got so bad that after the appearance of capitalist ideas and the Industrial Revolution, it still wasn't clear where God fit into the money system—or, more important, where money fit into God's system. Many religious leaders in Europe tended to gravitate to the new teachings of Karl Marx, whose theories were entirely centered on greed and hatred, and, most of all, atheism. They fanned the fires of covetousness, essentially telling people their whole problem was someone else. People were told that they were poor because the rich stole from them.

Now, in some cases it was true that the rich had stolen from the poor—but that was not the *cause* of their poverty. The cause was a spirit of poverty that was based on greed. It's a zero-sum game: a person can only get better off by making someone else worse off. That's not God. God doesn't need to make Sally worse off to improve your living standard. God has more than enough to enrich *both* you and Sally. But once you have the knowledge of the Word, you have no excuse. God will hold you accountable, and prosperity won't operate in your life without God.

Over these centuries, the notion that wealth was corrupting seemed to make some sense. After all, if you looked at most of the kings and nobles, a lot of them were pretty debauched. No one spoke in a clear voice to defend why God wanted His children prosperous. Pope Leo XIII gave it a try, in *Rerum Novarum* (1891), but he still got a lot wrong.[9] He did a good job of explaining why the doctrines of communism were empty, but that didn't help people understand how they personally could become more prosperous. It was just an older, more official sounding version of "hold on to God's unchanging hand."

If Christians don't stand up and explain God's system and how it works, rest assured the devil will provide an alternative explanation. Some of his lies will even sound plausible, and some may in fact resemble the real thing. After all, if you are going to counterfeit money, you don't counterfeit a three-dollar bill. That's because there is no such thing. It would be spotted immediately. Satan is smart enough to copy and pervert the things of God by making them look like the original, but with key ingredients missing.

For example, in America in the 1800s, you began to see rich business people, such as Andrew Carnegie, talking about something called the Gospel of Wealth. It sounded good: rich people should help out the less fortunate. They had an obligation to do so. Carnegie practiced what he preached—as I said, he gave away well over $350 million in his lifetime. But the Gospel of Wealth was a system without God. Poor people were not told how to obtain wealth on their own, and, more important, weren't told what role God plays in prosperity. Rather, the Gospel of Wealth almost encouraged them to rely on rich people. Rich folk liked it because it could soothe their consciences when they gave away money. It allowed them to feel better temporarily because they never had to come to grips with the fact that what was missing in their lives was God. One of the worst things was that the Gospel of Wealth reinforced the view that man got prosperity through his own (often shady) business talents, not from God. The devil had done an excellent job concealing the nature of riches, the principles of prosperity, and the life of abundance from most Christians.

We didn't get a change in these deceptions until some fifty years ago, when Oral Roberts first broke through into mainstream Christianity by emphasizing the healing promised to believers through our new covenant. Once ministers started to look at healing and began to see that it was indeed a promise—something all Christians had a right to—they began to look for other rights under our covenant. Only then did you start to see people discovering that prosperity on God's terms was one of those rights. The devil had succeeded for almost two thousand years keeping this quiet, but he couldn't keep it quiet any longer.

CHRISTIAN CREDIBILITY

Certainly the world's system did not disappear, but for the first time in hundreds of years, ministers of the gospel had finally gotten around to discerning God's plan for prosperity. Of course, anyone who stands up and tells people about this system better himself be living it. If I appear on national television and tell people about God's plan for them to prosper, I shouldn't look like a bum, with raggedy clothes. If I drove a broken-down heap, then what kind of credibility would I have? It's easy to see this with other aspects of God's kingdom; I don't know why it's so difficult to apply this principle to finances. For example, if a minister is teaching sexual purity but is out running around with a bunch of prostitutes, he would have zero credibility. If a preacher is advocating sobriety then is exposed as a drunk, no one will listen to him.

It's the same thing with prosperity. How in the world can I have credibility with you about handling your finances unless my own finances are impeccable? How can I encourage you to live prosperously if I'm living hand-to-mouth? Yet the minute a man or woman of God gets any kind of wealth, the wolves are at the door! Some people immediately assume that the preacher is stealing from the offering! "I'm not going to send my money to no preacher!" You hear that all the time, and it reveals utter ignorance of how God's system works.

You aren't my source. God is my source. I'd have it whether you sent it or not, because I've been faithful to what I've been called to do. This kind of thinking is that old poverty mentality—that wealth comes from man—and it's more of that old fear demon whispering that if you give it away, it's gone for good. For this reason, I made it up in my mind many years ago I can't be concerned with what you think about my suits, my watch, or my car. God gave me these things to enjoy, and I'm going to enjoy them.

People don't see that my wife and I tithe 40 percent of our income. We've been tithing for over thirty years and haven't missed a week. *That's* why we are prosperous—because we've been faithful. So someone sees me on television and says, "Why should I give my money to that preacher? He doesn't need it!" You're right, I don't need it, but you're heart is wrong. You aren't giving it to me anyway. And, just so you don't forget, it isn't *your* money in the first place—it's God's. I didn't command you to bring the tithe into the storehouse, God did. If you have a problem, take it up with Him.

I can't speak to what any other minister does with his or her finances. I'm not called to audit their books or be a policeman of their actions. I'm called to give an account of my ministry, my finances, the finances of Crenshaw Christian Centers and Ever Increasing Faith Ministries, and they are spotless. We have regular audits and don't even have the slightest appearance of impropriety, but that doesn't stop the critics, who don't understand how God's system works. For example, a few months ago, a national television network ran a nighttime news program that quoted me out of context and tried to make it look like I was bragging about having a yacht, cars, and so on. I don't even own a yacht—I was making a point about good success versus bad success. But that didn't stop this show. Certainly the producers didn't take the time to even listen to my whole message and try to understand how God's prosperity system works. And, they certainly did not interview me or any other Christian who has worked God's plan successfully.

GOOD SUCCESS VS. BAD SUCCESS

This is what we face on a daily basis. The devil uses every means at his disposal to convince Christians that they need to be poor, that they can't get ahead, or that if they do follow God's program, all they will do is enrich "fat cat" ministers. Satan has another trick up his sleeve, too. He elevates all sorts of rich people into the public eye who obtain their money from sin. Whether it's rappers, pornographers, athletes, corrupt business people, or politicians, every day you can open a newspaper and see numerous examples of the rich and famous who are anything but godly. There is a television series dedicated to a famous pornographer and his three live-in sex partners, which celebrates how much money they spend on clothes, parties, and general hedonism. MTV has a show on the "cribs" of famous music stars and rappers, emphasizing the opulence and luxury in which they live.

Joshua 1:8, however, says there are prerequisites to prospering:

> This Book of the Law shall not depart from your mouth, but you shall meditate in it day and night, that you may observe to do according to all that is written in it. For then you will make your way prosperous, and then you will have good success.

Note that if you do these things, you will have good success. Well, what is "bad" success? If you had $27 million in the bank, owned five houses free and clear, and had seven autos parked in front of your house, plus a jet airplane and a yacht, the world would call you a success. But while you had those things, if your wife or husband was running around with someone else, if your kids were on drugs, if you couldn't trust any of your friends because you never knew if they were after your money or not, and if your stomach was torn up with ulcers worrying about your portfolio, then you'd have bad success.

Good success is when you get your wealth the right way, can sleep at night, are at peace with God, and walk beside His "still waters." Let me show you something in Proverbs 10:22: "The blessing of the LORD makes one rich, And He adds no sorrow with it." If your wealth is bringing you sorrow, it's not from the Lord. But look at this verse again: "The blessing of the LORD makes one rich." Remember, this promise is found in the old covenant, and this blessing meant *physical and material riches*, so you have to pay someone to help you misunderstand this verse. God will bless you with physical and material blessings, and they don't come with negative side effects. Money itself is never a problem; it is a blessing, if it comes from God.

However, if money comes from the devil's system, you can appear prosperous for a season, but the end is destruction. Look at some of the people who this world calls successful. Examine any book of, say, Hollywood stars between 1960 and 1990; you can count the number who stayed married to the same person on one hand. Success that comes from the devil—*even if it doesn't appear like he's the source of your success*—will never be good success. How many times has Britney Spears, once considered a superstar, been in rehab? How many famous comedians—people with money that the world equates with laughter and happiness—have either killed themselves or died of drug overdoses? It's a long list! Unless wealth comes God's way, it will always be bad success. Hebrews 11:25 tells us that there are, indeed, "passing pleasures of sin." But seasons come and go, and "God is not mocked" (Gal. 6:7). Sooner or later, whether it's through your health, your family's well-being, your mental stability, or your relationships, the devil will present his bill. His payment will come due, and it will bring you sorrow.

With God, however, you can have prosperity and a clean conscience. Again, Jesus said, "Give, and it will be given to you" (Luke 6:38). One of the mysteries of God's plan is that the more you give away to the kingdom of God, the more you will receive. Arthur Brooks, a professor of public administration at Syracuse University, wrote an amazing book called *Who Really Cares?* It's a study of Americans' philanthropy: who gives, why, and what the results are. Some of his findings, while not at all surprising to those of us who have preached tithing and giving as a means to activate God's prosperity, are worth noting. He claims, "There is no doubt that prosperity and charity are positively correlated.... An average American family earning one hundred thousand dollars or more in the year 2000 was ten percentage points more likely to give to charity and gave a larger percentage of its household income than an average lower middle-class family earning between thirty thousand and fifty thousand dollars."[10] Want to talk about good success? Brooks found that "givers are 25 percent more likely than non-givers to say their health is excellent or very good."[11] And while it's not all tithing, Brooks reported that "people who give money in a charitable fashion are 43 percent more likely to say they are 'very happy' than nongivers; and nongivers are three and a half times more likely than givers to say they are 'not happy at all.'"[12]

You get the picture. Jesus wasn't kidding when He said, "Give, and it will be given to you." God meant it in Joshua when He said if you put Him first, you will have good success. He will make sure that your prosperity does not come at the expense of your happiness, your relationships, your family, or your peace of mind.

Notes

Notes

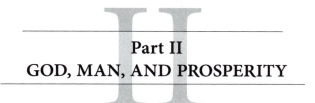

Part II
GOD, MAN, AND PROSPERITY

Chapter 6
THE PROSPERITY PIPELINE

S O FAR, WE'VE proven without doubt that God is not poor. He has a plan for our prosperity, established through Abraham and the old covenant, and we have seen that we are the legal heirs to that covenant. We have seen that there is a law of tithes and offerings—it's not an option. This law was instituted long before the Ten Commandments, and it is one of those laws that did not disappear with the institution of the new covenant. The law of tithing involves the scriptural principle of sowing and reaping and contains penalties for robbing God. When you bring your tithes into the storehouse, you are to take care which storehouse you bring them to, because you are not to pay tithe to a dead church.

We have also seen that we have a better covenant with the Lord Jesus Christ and that we have certain rights in His covenant. Those rights include all of the promises of Deuteronomy, as well as spiritual blessings that those under the old covenant could not provide because Jesus had not yet completed His redemptive work.

Finally, we've seen that there is a competing prosperity system with God's system—the world's approach to prosperity, which is driven by a spirit of poverty. Satan's goal is to get as many people as possible depending on the world's system so that he can ensnare them in a poverty trap. His system is based on greed and fear, mirror images of each other that tell people they'll never have enough, regardless of how rich they are. And we've seen that there is good success and bad success. In the latter case, it's entirely possible for a person to be prosperous financially, yet have all other aspects of his or her life coming apart as the payment the devil extracts for making them rich. Satan's system depends on ignorance and lies, convincing people that God wants them poor, so as to make it harder for people to come to Him.

God's will—and we already established that we can know His will—is to prosper His children. Even Job, whom we saw earlier get a few things wrong, got this part right:

> Behold, God is mighty, but despises no one; He is mighty in strength of understanding. He does not preserve the life of the wicked, But gives justice to the oppressed. He does not withdraw His eyes from the righteous; But they are on the throne with kings, For He has seated them forever, And they are exalted. And if they are bound in fetters, held in the cords of affliction, Then He tells them their work and their transgressions—that they have acted defiantly. He also opens their ear to instruction, and commands that they turn from iniquity. If they obey and serve Him, they shall spend their days in prosperity, and their years in pleasure.
>
> —Job 36:5–11

These verses inform us that God is not opposed to me or you prospering. But again, notice the prerequisites. We have to live a godly life in order to spend our days in prosperity. That's old covenant, you say. Look at 3 John 2: "Beloved, I pray that you may prosper in all things and be in health, just as your soul prospers." John is from the new covenant, right? And here he makes it impossible to mess up by saying, "I pray that you may prosper in all things *and* be in

144

health, *just as your soul prospers.*" If by "prospering" John meant something spiritual, he wouldn't add the phrase "and be in health," which is physical, then say "just as your soul prospers." So whatever "prospering" John meant, it was in addition to your soul prospering, meaning it has to be material and not spiritual.

Remember that the Old Testament verses quoted above refer *only* to physical and material things. When it says, "They shall spend their days in prosperity" (Job 36:11), obviously it refers to our living our daily lives, because you won't have "days" when you are with God in eternity. Salvation is the beginning, not the end, of the blessings. Jesus said in John 10:10, "The thief does not come except to steal, and to kill, and to destroy. I have come that they may have life, and that they may have it more abundantly." Many churches for years have taught that getting saved was all there was to the Christian life. After that, it's "hold on to God's unchanging hand!" If getting saved were *all* that it was about—and I will agree with you that it is *numero uno*—then every Christian would die immediately after professing Jesus as the Lord of his or her life. What's the point of living? Jesus said it clearly: "That you may have [life] more abundantly" (John 10:10).

In Matthew 6:33, Jesus instructed us, "But seek first the kingdom of God and His righteousness, and all these things shall be added to you." All what? All these *things*. What things was He talking about? He had just finished the passage about worry, where He said not to worry about clothes, or houses, or food—in other words, physical, material things. Note that He did not say, "Seek first the kingdom of God and all these spiritual blessings will be added to you!" If you already have Jesus and you are saved, you are already spiritually blessed. How much more spiritually blessed can you get? No, these things that would be added were indeed material things. Stuff. Daily necessities and, yes, luxuries. Note that He didn't even say, "All the necessary things would be added to you." He didn't qualify it at all. To God, the things make no difference. He's a wealthy God, remember? In terms of His pure wealth, the richest man on earth is like the poorest Third World beggar.

There is another little gem in Matthew 6:33. Did you notice that Jesus said that those things would be "added" to you? Things can't possibly be bad in and of themselves if they are "added." Otherwise, He would have said, "Seek first…and these things will be subtracted from you!" Moreover, look at Who is doing the adding: God. I have a question for you. How can God add anything bad to your life? Remember, Job said God took away from him, but we know now that God does not take away.

Let's go back to the rich young ruler. After the young man went away sad: "Then Jesus looked around and said to His disciples, 'How hard it is for those who have riches to enter the kingdom of God!' And the disciples were astonished at His words. But Jesus answered again and said to them, 'Children, how hard it is for those who trust in riches to enter the kingdom of God!'" (Mark 10:23–24). A reasonable question might be, why in the world would the disciples be "astonished" that Jesus said it was hard for rich people to get into heaven if they—like many today—had always heard that the rich people were evil? The disciples were astonished for two reasons. First, many of them, while perhaps not as rich as this young ruler, were well off. As we'll see in another section, Peter and James had a fishing business with boats and servants; Peter had a house big enough to live with his wife and mother-in-law (and you married people know that was a *big* house!); and Matthew was a tax collector who got 10 percent of every tax dollar that came across his table for his services. These were not poor men. Perhaps they weren't what we'd call ultra rich, but they were middle class in Galilean terms. They were stunned that Jesus *seemed* to imply that they might not get into the kingdom. Second, they knew the promises of Abraham. They knew the blessings that were promised to the obedient Jews, and I'm sure these men thought they'd been obedient.

So on two counts, it stunned them that Jesus seemed to say that no rich person could get into heaven. Obviously, Jesus knew they had missed the boat because He repeated the same comment, but this time with emphasis: "Children, how hard it is for those who *trust in riches* to enter the kingdom of God!" (Mark 10:24). It wasn't about the riches; it was about the trust. Who do you trust? Your money or your God?

GOD CAN USE CIRCUMSTANCES TO "TEACH"—BUT HE WOULD RATHER USE HIS WORD

Money and health are two areas of the Bible that people seem to have a great deal of trouble with. How many times have you heard someone say, "The Lord put this on me (pick your disease here) to teach me a lesson"? Or, "My (cancer/rheumatism/diabetes) was actually a blessing from God, because it changed my life." If that were true—that God teaches us and blesses us through sickness and disease—then what does God have against all those Christians who are not sick? Shouldn't we all pray for cancer if that's how we learn and grow? No! It's a lie of the devil that God gives His people diseases and makes them poor to teach them anything. Remember Proverbs 10:22, which I quoted in an earlier chapter: "The blessing of the LORD makes one rich, And He adds no sorrow with it." Combine that with James 1:17, "Every good gift and every perfect gift is from above, and comes down from the Father of lights, with whom there is no variation or shadow of turning." "No sorrow." "Every good and perfect gift." Where in the world does anyone get poverty or sickness out of that?

It is absolutely true that God can and will *use* your circumstances to teach you if you are so hardheaded you cannot learn from His Word. But God's best is that you learn from the Word. Second Timothy 3:16–17 says: "All Scripture is given by inspiration of God, and is profitable for doctrine, for reproof, for correction, for instruction in righteousness, that the man of God may be complete, thoroughly equipped for every good work." How many times do we see these phrases, "every good work," "every good and every perfect gift," "no sorrow," and "more abundantly"? Do you think God is trying to tell us something? I do. There is no sickness and no poverty in God the Father. He cannot give you what He doesn't have.

Jesus did not wish the rich young ruler to be the poor, old, sick beggar. Jesus healed every person He came in contact with—every single one—who *asked* to be healed. Further, man's faith is a part of that, which is why Jesus just didn't walk down the street and people got healed. The sick and oppressed had to exercise their faith. Neither can Jesus just give you abundant life if you don't accept it. Your free will is involved.

But I want to examine a different aspect of this rich young ruler to show you something you probably haven't thought of before. Notice that when he asked what he had to do to inherit eternal life, Jesus told him to keep the commandments. In Mark 10:20, we see that the young man answered, "Teacher, all these things I have kept from my youth." Jesus then told him to "go your way, sell whatever you have and give to the poor, and you will have treasure in heaven; and come, take up the cross, and follow Me" (Mark 10:21). By the way, Matthew and Luke's use of the term "give to the poor" did not mean "give everything you have to the poor," because then you would be poor as well. The verse means to begin to live a life of giving. At any rate, we have already seen that the riches, in this fellow's case, were a stumbling block to him. However, here is the point I want to make: when the man said he had kept those commandments, Jesus—who certainly knew the man's heart if He knew nothing else—did *not* say "You're a liar! You haven't kept these commandments." I think this is a very important point.

Many who do studies on this story and its companion renditions in Luke and Matthew either completely gloss over this or they say, "Of course this man had not kept the commandments! No one could." In the new context of the *spirit* as well as the *letter* of the law that Jesus had outlined in Matthew 5, the man could not possibly have kept the law. Assume this man had not heard all of Jesus' teachings, however, and that he had obeyed the old covenant to the utmost of his ability. Is there a way Jesus could have known that without being able to look into his soul? Yes. The man was rich. He was displaying the very blessing of Abraham that had been promised for those who were obedient. Jesus didn't call the man a liar precisely because he *had* kept the strict letter of the law and it had made him prosperous.

It's the same reason the disciples were astonished at Jesus' teaching. In Mark 10:25 and 27, He said "It is easier for a camel to go through the eye of a needle than for a rich man to enter into the kingdom of God.... But Jesus looked at them and said, 'With men it is impossible, but not with God; for with God all things are possible.'" So I have a question for you: which do you think is more difficult for God, saving a poor person or saving a rich person? The answer is, it's the same, regardless, for God. He has the power, regardless. It's the *person* for whom the wealth makes a difference. It's obviously possible with God for a camel to go through the eye of a needle. God has made planets vastly larger than Earth (Jupiter, for example). Imagine if you had a needle's eye on Jupiter that was sized proportionately. It would be plenty large for an earthly camel to go through.

For many years, ministers and Sunday school teachers have claimed there was a gate in Jerusalem called the Eye of the Needle that was smaller than other gates and through which a camel could go if it got down on its knees. The message was that if Christians are sufficiently humble and come before God without baggage, we can enter the kingdom of God. Unfortunately, this is a myth. There is no record of such a gate. Rather, the term "eye of the needle" is used in Jewish literature to symbolize that God only needs a tiny opening with which to work. One Jewish midrash says, "The Holy One said, open for me a door as big as a needle's eye and I will open for you a door through which may enter tents and [camels];" while another says "A needle's eye is not too narrow for two friends, but the world is not wide enough for two enemies."[1]

What's clear about all this is that it isn't the riches that stand in all men's way, but what stood in *this particular man's way*. The man went away sad because "he had great possessions" (Mark 10:22), but as I have shown you before, the truth was that the great possessions had him.

Modern Christians who advocate a socialist economic structure, such as *Sojourners* magazine, love to indict all riches through this verse. It is abundantly clear to any honest person who looks at this that Jesus was making a much larger point about any possession or relationship that gets between you and Him, *not* just money. Money was the young ruler's problem.

Money Isn't the Only Impediment to Following Jesus

In Matthew 8:21, we see that another man who had followed Jesus, apparently for some time, said "Lord, let me first go and bury my father." Jesus answered, "Follow Me, and let the dead bury their own dead" (Matt. 8:22). Once again, the Lord's point was that following Him should be the first priority. We see in Luke 9:61, another said, "Lord, I will follow You, but let me first go and bid them farewell who are at my house." Jesus responded, "No one, having put his hand to the plow, and looking back, is fit for the kingdom of God" (v. 62). Now, we know that Jesus Himself went back to His hometown of Nazareth, so that wasn't the problem. The whole issue, in all three of these cases, is the condition these men put on their service. They were saying, "Yes, I will follow you, *but....*"

With one, the *but* was money; with another, his dead father; and with a third, saying good-bye to his family. We have no evidence at all that Jesus was insensitive to these needs. Rather, He needed followers who would put Him and His kingdom first.

Over and above all this, if you think God didn't want you to have something, couldn't He arrange it so you lost it all? Merely depriving the man of money would not have accomplished anything, because he still would have been fixated on wealth. The man had to put Jesus first. In Luke 12:51–54 Jesus put it another way:

> Do you suppose that I came to give peace on earth?
> I tell you, not at all, but rather division. For from now
> on five in one house will be divided: three against two,
> and two against three. Father will be divided against
> son and son against father, mother against daughter
> and daughter against mother, mother-in-law against
> her daughter-in-law and daughter-in-law against her
> mother-in-law.

The point wasn't that Jesus wanted people to be in conflict. Quite the contrary—Paul told us to "live peaceably with all men" if it is possible, as much as depends on you (Rom. 12:18)— but Jesus did predict that completely selling out for Him would divide families. Notice back in the account of the rich young ruler that Jesus said, "Come, take up the cross, and follow Me." Now, Jesus had not yet been crucified, so this clearly did not mean that He was telling the man to die for Him. Rather, He was making it uncomfortable for the man. Not only did He ask him to give up his wealth, but to travel with Jesus, leaving family, friends, and the comforts of his home.

Did other people do that? Yes. After Jesus told the disciples how hard it was for a rich man to enter the kingdom of God, Peter in Matthew 19:27 said, "See, we have left all and followed You. Therefore what shall we have?" Note that even then, Peter's heart wasn't quite right. He was asking a reasonable question, "Look, Lord, if the bad guys who don't follow you have all the money, what do we get?" But by then Peter should have *known* what he had. Even if Peter had nothing else in his life, he had the love and trust of Jesus the Messiah, who would constantly select Peter out for special experiences. How much is that worth?

Yet again, Jesus did *not* say that, even though it was true. Matthew 19:28–30 contain the answer Jesus gave them:

So Jesus said to them, "Assuredly I say to you, that in the regeneration, when the Son of Man sits on the throne of His glory, you who have followed Me will also sit on twelve thrones, judging the twelve tribes of Israel. And everyone who has left houses or brothers or sisters or father or mother or wife or children or lands, for My name's sake, shall receive a hundredfold, and inherit eternal life."

Mark's translation is even more stunning, and some of the small differences have profound implications:

So Jesus answered and said, "Assuredly, I say to you, there is no one who has left house or brothers or sisters or father or mother or wife or children or lands, for My sake and the gospel's, who shall not receive a hundred-fold now in this time—houses and brothers and sisters and mothers and children and lands, with persecutions—and in the age to come, eternal life."

—Mark 10:29–30

Both say that believers will inherit eternal life in the next world, and both say that believers will receive a hundredfold return—which I will discuss in a later chapter. What is interesting is how Mark makes it clear that all of these blessings are "now in this time" (v. 30). Jesus then spelled it out, including "and lands." Land was the main source of wealth back then. If you had land, you could sell it for gold and silver.

SHOULD CHRISTIANS SUFFER POVERTY "FOR THE LORD"?

How can anyone mess this up? Based on all the evidence we have discussed so far, how do you come to any other conclusion except that "in this time" we are to be wealthy—with persecutions. As I have discussed in a book called *Why Should Christians Suffer?* the concept of persecution is almost always assumed by Christians to be physical pain and suffering, and Jesus never meant it that way.[2] We can never, ever replicate the suffering that Jesus went through and can't even empathize with it, because His *real* suffering, as horrible as the flogging and the cross were, was His separation from the Father when He took on the sin of the world. We can't know that and have no clue what that involved. Moreover, as I pointed out in that book, Jesus was never, ever sick. He never had a cold, never had diabetes, and never got cancer. People criticized Him and threatened Him, but not one time did anyone *ever* lay a hand on the Lord. We have many instances where He walked right through crowds, disappeared from their midst, or otherwise kept them from even touching Him. So when He said we would all suffer persecutions and when Paul said we would partake in His suffering, we need to know how He suffered. He wasn't sick. He wasn't physically beaten up by the Pharisees, and no one could touch Him until the last days where His mission called for Him to be offered up. Jesus said of His life, "No one takes it from Me, but I lay it down of Myself. I have power to lay it down, and I have power to take it again. This command I have received from the Father" (John 10:18).

Jesus willingly gave His life to do what we could not, namely save all men from sin. Neither you nor I can accomplish one thing in the kingdom by dying. It's interesting that a whole school of teaching on martyrs has developed from the early church fathers, yet none of it was included in the Bible. In other words, many of these people who died were brave people, to be greatly admired for their love of the Lord, but their interpretation of what was required of them was wrong. Even the word *martyr* means "witness," and you sure don't have to be fed to hungry lions to be a witness for Christ. In fact, when you're gone, I who am alive will still be witnessing!

Jesus made it clear that we would not lose anything except ourselves if we followed Him—that He would see that we were compensated for our commitment to His Word in *this life*. Well, let's ask a question: was Jesus married? No. So He couldn't lose a wife. Did He have a father? Yes, but although the Bible doesn't say, it's apparent by Joseph's absence that he died before Jesus began His earthly ministry. Did He have a mother? Oh, yes He did. Did He lose her? I don't think so. Look at John 19:26. On the cross, Jesus "saw His mother, and the disciple whom He loved standing by, [and] He said to His mother, 'Woman, behold your son!'" Jesus obviously didn't lose His mother if right up until the grim end He addressed her affectionately and saw to her care and well-being. The Bible states clearly she was His mother, so that relationship had never changed.

As we have seen, Peter had a wife. He obviously left her from time to time to travel with Jesus, but 1 Corinthians 9:5, thought by most scholars to be written before the Gospels, has Paul asking a rhetorical question of the Corinthians: "Do we have no right to take along a believing wife, as do also the other apostles, the brothers of the Lord, and Cephas?" Cephas, of course, was Peter, so he was traveling with his "believing wife." Obviously even though those disciples "gave up" their wives, they didn't lose them permanently.

Lest someone say that Jesus was endorsing polygamy, let's establish that He was not. Nor was He promising that you would get one hundred children if you followed Him. Who in the world wants one hundred kids? Most people have a tough enough time raising two or three. Most married men would tell you they can barely keep one woman happy, let alone five. Solomon, who had seven hundred wives and three hundred concubines, gave us this timeless assessment of how that worked out: "Vanity of vanities. It's all vanity" (Eccles. 1:2). Some people might say, "I wish I had twenty cars—a different car for every mood." Very quickly you'd find that you only drive one or two, and the rest would sit in a garage, collecting dust and forcing you to hire someone to wash them on a regular basis.

Jesus meant that whoever had given up their life to focus on the Lord would be blessed a hundred times over. It's an expression, meaning that the blessings are given in abundance—they just don't end. Consider the American missionary who leaves all and goes to New Guinea. Perhaps his wife accompanies him, but he has left his mother, perhaps children, and certainly his house. His brothers and sisters, who likely are not in the ministry, stay in America. Yet after a short time of witnessing to the people in New Guinea, he finds he and his wife are welcomed and loved by the tribes. The older women of the tribes treat him as though he were their son, and his wife as their daughter. Could you say he gained one hundred mothers? I think so. And the younger women of the tribe perhaps bring him food and look up to him like a father. Could you say he gained one hundred daughters? Or that the young men who bring him along to hunt or transport him on their boats—are they not like his sons? No, they are not blood-kin, but he has gained many times more the *relationships* of those he left behind. He may not have his own home, but he and his wife are welcome in any of the villagers' homes, where he would be given the "master bedroom," such as it is.

Don't get all concerned and think, "I don't want to go to Africa or Latin America or the South Sea Islands! Even the master bedroom of a hut isn't as good as my little bedroom." God will not ask you to do something He knows isn't in your heart to do anyway. The point is God won't let you come up short. But here's the key, the "trick" if you will: for you to gain everything, you must be willing to give up everything. Not flippantly or insincerely, but genuinely willing to "seek first the kingdom of God and His righteousness" (Matt. 6:33). That's the requirement. *Then* "all these things shall be added" to you. Until you get to that point where you can say, like Peter, "Lord I've left everything for you," even if only in your heart, then you cannot expect the promises of God to be added to you.

The Transfer of Wealth: Challenges, Questions, and Solutions

So, how does this transfer of wealth work? There has to be more to it than saying, "Lord, everything I have is yours," then sitting and waiting. And you're right. There are some basic steps you must do to activate God's prosperity.

First, tithe. Tithing is the first step of obedience that enables God to bless you. This is true if you have a lot or have a little. In Luke 16:10 Jesus said, "He who is faithful in what is least is faithful also in much; and he who is unjust in what is least is unjust also in much." Why should God trust you with one hundred thousand dollars a year if you can't tithe on twenty thousand dollars a year? It's God's form of training. Other versions, including the New American Standard, use the word *dishonest* instead of *unjust*. That's pretty accurate, in that it is an issue of honesty—"Will a man rob God?" (Mal. 3:8).

Let's deal with some reality, though, shall we? Many of you are in debt up to your eyeballs. You sincerely don't want to rob God, but before you came into a knowledge of tithing, you had already fouled up your finances. You owe "the Man!" If you don't pay your bills, you are violating contracts. For every one of those credit card bills you have, at one point you signed your name to a piece of paper promising in a contract to pay your debts and to pay them on time. What do you do? Pay God or pay man? If you pay God but default, you will be giving a false witness. There is a way to do both.

What I counsel people to do is this: pay what you can. Contact your creditor and explain that you intend to pay them. If you didn't know about tithing when you got into this, pay your debt. As soon as that bill is paid off, take that amount which was once due that company and give it to the Lord. And so on with the next bill, until you are tithing 10 percent. If it's me, I'm going to do everything I can to pay the tithe first. If you have to, open a bank account for your tithe money. Here is how I did it. I allowed Uncle Sam to save for me. I changed the status of my dependents for a year and claimed no dependents, even though I had four. At the end of the year, I claimed all my dependents back and got a refund, which I used to pay off a bill. I started tithing at that point and have never stopped since.

When Betty and I decided to get out of the financial rat race we were in, we made a pact that we would not buy anything we didn't absolutely need. We would not put anything on a credit card, except for in life-or-death situations. We stopped buying—we didn't even buy a Christmas tree for a couple of years. It was painful. But our commitment to do God's Word has liberated us, and today we live financially free.

Remember, your tithe should come off the top of your net paycheck—the first thing. I say net paycheck, because some people teach you need to tithe off the gross. Well, you don't have any control over that money that the government takes out of your check. In most cases, you don't even see that money. However, if you have arranged with the credit union to have your new car payment taken off the top of your paycheck, then that is money you are receiving and you must tithe off that amount, as well. You don't tithe from what's left over after your expenses; you live on what's left over after the tithe. Train yourself so that whenever you see one hundred dollars, you really see it as ninety dollars. Automatically, you think, "OK, God gets the first 10 percent." Keep asking yourself this question: *If you were God, would you trust you?*

Another issue that frequently arises is among couples who are unequally yoked. What if you are married to a spouse that, perhaps, is a Christian but who doesn't believe in tithing? What do you do? You've spoken to him about it, but it's clear he doesn't think tithing is "for us today." My advice to you is for you to tithe on what you receive as income. Say he gives you two hundred dollars a month for your personal needs: nails, hair, clothes, or whatever. You tithe your twenty dollars out of that. God will honor that.

In 2 Corinthians 6:14, Paul wrote "Do not be unequally yoked together with unbelievers. For what fellowship has righteousness with lawlessness? And what communion has light with darkness?" First and foremost, this is a scripture about marriage, but *unbelievers* doesn't just mean "not believing in Christ." It is part of the Prayer of Agreement we see in Matthew 18:19, when Jesus said, "Again I say to you that if two of you agree on earth concerning anything that they ask, it will be done for them by My Father in heaven."

So you have to agree on whatever it is you are praying and believing for. If your mate doesn't believe in tithing, you can destroy your marriage trying to force that issue. It's the same thing in business. Even two Christian brothers and sisters who are partners in a firm better be in agreement. If one of you believes that God will bless your business and the other believes that "whatever will be, will be," then you have a problem. Again, my advice on being yoked to someone who doesn't believe in tithing is to only tithe on what is yours.

Ultimately, unless you are giving 10 percent, fifty-two weeks a year, you are not a tither. You may be giving to your church, but you are not a tither. And remember when we looked at tithes and offerings, we noted that God loves a "cheerful" giver. When I write the check for my tithe, I am saying, "Father, I honor You; I worship You with this act of faith. I am separating me from that which I earned through the labor, the sweat, as it were, of my brow. I am giving this to You Father; I'm paying my debt to You gladly, happily. Thank You for blessing me so much that I can do it."

I was not always in a position to say this. When I was robbing God in years gone by, I couldn't get a handle on anything. I don't care how much money I made, it never seemed to be enough. It got so bad that I had to declare bankruptcy. They repossessed my television, the car, called back all the credit cards. Me—a minister of the gospel—bankrupt! I loved God with all my heart, but I was operating in that curse and did not even know it.

Our first ingredient for prosperity is obedience. The second ingredient is to let God know what it is you want or need. You may want a Maserati, but if you never told anyone that, even if people could get you a wonderful gift, they would never think to buy you a Maserati. It is true that God knows what you need and want—He knows the hidden recesses of your heart. But activating the blessings of God in your life comes back to free will. For God to just "peek into your soul" and provide everything would take the element of free will out of it. Therefore, in prayer, you must ask for what you want. Jesus said in Matthew 21:21–22:

> Assuredly, I say unto you, if you have faith and do not doubt, you will not only do what was done to the fig tree, but also if you say to this mountain, "Be removed and cast into the sea," it will be done. And whatever things you ask in prayer, believing, you will receive.

If you are tithing and are not receiving any blessings back, you might want to do a self-check: have I ever bothered to *ask* God for this or that? Don't be too clever and ask for some generic blessing thinking that God will just fill in the blanks. Let your petitions be known to God. In Philippians 4:6, Paul wrote "Be anxious for nothing, but in everything by prayer and supplication, with thanksgiving, let your requests be made known to God." If you aren't willing to ask, God cannot answer.

You might notice another condition of asking stated in Matthew 21:22, which is that whatever you ask in prayer, "believing," you will receive. Faith is a key ingredient of this process. That's why God wants you to ask—it's a means of checking your faith. It's not enough to ask and hope. You must ask and believe you receive it. That begins by under-standing deep in your heart that God wants you to be blessed. You won't believe it, and you sure won't ask for it if you think God wants you poor. I've been rich, and I've been poor; and rich is better. But don't take it from me—take it from Chris Gardner, the man who Will Smith played in the hit movie, *The Pursuit of Happyness*. Here was a man who with his little boy was homeless, living in shelters, and sleeping on the BART system in San Francisco. He eventually became a highly successful stockbroker and bond trader, opening his own business and making millions of dollars. In his book, *The Pursuit of Happyness*, he wrote that he thought he'd never have a care in the world after he made money, but he found out differently:

> Well, of course, as I later would learn, it doesn't work like that. Anyone who believes that money saves all has never had any money—like me back then.... What I would discover was that while money is better to have than not to have, it not only doesn't fix all the problems but brings with it problems that [I] couldn't have imagined [when I didn't have it].[3]

Now, I didn't have problems when I got money because I had already learned that lesson. If you know that God is the source of your money and honor Him with it, you will have no problems. Remember Proverbs 10:22, "The blessing of the Lord makes one rich, And He adds no sorrow with it."

Finally, if you have gotten into the tithing habit and you are identifying your needs and desires and asking God for them in faith, it is assured you will be blessed abundantly. You must keep your heart right, however. God is not so stupid as to turn over wads of greenbacks to someone who will blow it at the racetrack. You have a purpose for your prosperity. Remember, "Give, and it shall be given to you" (Luke 6:38). God wants you in such a financial situation *and mental state* that you are a giving machine. My wife Betty has her own checking account just for giving to special needs. That's above and beyond her tithe. Can God count on you to give? Are you faithful in little? I'm a connoisseur of fine neckties. To me, a necktie makes a great suit. Suppose I purchase a wonderful tie—and a good, silk tie can go for seventy-five, one hundred, or two hundred dollars if you get a quality tie—and one of the staff walks by and says, "Pastor that is a fantastic tie!" The Spirit inside says, "Bless that man with your tie." What do I do? Give him my tie. Many people would lay out a fleece, wait for the sun to darken, or pray for a word from the Lord. But you *know* if He has put something on your heart.

Are you faithful in little? Do you give when you are supposed to—and, again, I'm not talking tithe here, because that isn't an option. Charitable giving must always be done carefully. Some people are scam artists and no more want to work for food than they want to listen to a rap version of "The Old Rugged Cross." You must use godly wisdom and guidance. Is someone hungry, or does he want to use the money for liquor? One way to handle that is to carry gift coupons from some of the fast food restaurants. If the person is truly hungry, that will be like gold. Otherwise, the person won't even take them from you.

If the Lord calls you to give, it is to open a new spigot to bless you! It may not even be something expensive, but something that you personally really treasure. Maybe it is a ring that a favorite aunt gave you. Maybe it's a one-of-a-kind recording of some music group that you got in a record shop. God can only measure back to you what you give. You will only reap what you sow, but the very first sowing you need to do is with your tithe to the Lord.

Notes

Notes

Chapter 7
THE PURPOSE OF PROSPERITY

G OD IS WEALTHY. He wants you to prosper. By following His simple rules, you will prosper. But for what reason? To what purpose?

There is a purpose for prosperity, and it is not for you to squander by living the big life. God's purposes are explained in John 6:38–40, where Jesus says:

> For I have come down from heaven, not to do My own will, but the will of Him who sent Me. This is the will of the Father who sent Me, that of all He has given Me I should lose nothing, but should raise it up at the last day. And this is the will of Him who sent Me, that everyone who sees the Son and believes in Him may have everlasting life; and I will raise him up on the last day.

According to this, God wills that everyone come into the knowledge of His Son Jesus Christ and receive Him so they can be saved. In that way, the relationship God had with man before the fall of Adam can be re-established.

We see again in Jesus' encounter with Zacchaeus:

> Then Jesus entered and passed through Jericho. Now behold, there was a man named Zacchaeus who was a chief tax collector, and he was rich. And he sought to see who Jesus was, but could not because of the crowd, for he was of short stature. So he ran ahead and climbed up into a sycamore tree to see Him, for He was going

167

to pass that way. And when Jesus came to the place, He looked up and saw him, and said to him, "Zacchaeus, make haste and come down, for today I must stay at your house." So he made haste and came down, and received Him joyfully. But when they saw it, they all complained, saying, "He has gone to be a guest with a man who is a sinner." Then Zacchaeus stood and said to the Lord, "Look, Lord, I give half of my goods to the poor; and if I have taken anything from anyone by false accusation, I restore fourfold." And Jesus said to him, "Today salvation has come to this house, because he also is a son of Abraham; for the Son of Man has come to seek and to save that which was lost."

—Luke 19:1–10

There is the will of God in a nutshell: "to seek and save that which was lost" (v. 10).

And did you notice the different attitudes in Zacchaeus and the rich young ruler we saw earlier? They were both rich. They were wealthy because they were sons of Abraham and had tithed and been obedient. But when faced with the Son of God, their responses were 180 degrees opposite. The rich young ruler went away sad because he didn't want to give away his possessions. Look at Zacchaeus—he didn't even wait for Jesus to say anything, nor did he even ask about salvation! He said, "Look, Lord, I give half my goods to the poor; and if I have taken anything from anyone by false accusation, I restore fourfold" (v. 8). Being a tax collector, there were almost certainly some questionable situations that arose, and since Zacchaeus worked for the Romans (as did Matthew), he likely resolved most of those disputes in favor of the government.

Zacchaeus got the point, without even being told. The honor of having the Son of God grace his house for dinner—you can imagine poor old Mrs. Zacchaeus was in a frenzy, cleaning and getting out the good dishes!—so humbled him that his first thought was, "I need to help other people," and his second thought was, "If I've wronged someone, I need to make it right." His heart was in the right place. He rightly understood that if things were going to get done in this world, it would be through the hands of man.

When Jesus was ready to go back to heaven, He said to His disciples, and ultimately to all of us who would come into the body of Christ and become His disciples, "Go into all the world and preach the gospel to every creature" (Mark 16:15). He didn't say, "Build a church and wait for the world to come to you." No, He said for us to go into the world. Jesus told Peter in Matthew 16:18, "And I also say to you that you are Peter, and on this rock I will build My church, and the gates of Hades shall not prevail against it." Notice that Jesus did not say that it was the church that had "gates," but rather Hades. It was clearly a reference to a movement that was on offense, and that not even the "gates," or strongholds, of hell would prevail against us.

Most Christians have the erroneous notion that the local church is for getting people saved. No! The local church is for the purpose of shepherding the "sheep" and the "lambs" to grow them up so they can seek the lost. Many Christians have made prosperity totally about themselves. They have better clothes, newer cars, more electronic toys, and bigger houses. But that prosperity exists for a reason: "to seek and to save that which was lost" (Luke 19:10). Prosperity exists to "go into all the world and preach the gospel to every creature" (Mark 16:15). When Jesus said in Matthew 6:33 to "seek first the kingdom of God," He didn't say "seek *only*" the kingdom. But if you seek God's kingdom first, your prosperity will always be directed toward the right end.

ARE YOU SHORTCHANGING GOD?

You might think that selfishness when it comes to God can't really be a factor if you are tithing. Yet even if you are tithing *and* giving offerings, you still might be shortchanging God if your attitude is based in a poverty mentality. For example, maybe you have made it up in your mind what is the level of giving to God that you find acceptable. Well, I find that unacceptable. We should *daily* look for ways to increase our prosperity for the purpose of increasing our giving. Ask yourself, *if I am all that God has to seek and save the lost, is God in trouble?* Where will the money come from to build hospitals, feed the hungry, and provide clothing so that you (or a missionary) will have an opportunity to tell someone about Jesus?

Jesus spoke about this in a parable in Luke 10:25–37:

> And behold, a certain lawyer stood up and tested Him, saying, "Teacher, what shall I do to inherit eternal life?" He said to him, "What is written in the law? What is your reading of it?" So he answered and said, "'You shall love the Lord your God with all your heart, with all your soul, with all your strength, and with all your mind,' and 'your neighbor as yourself.'" And He said to him, "You have answered rightly; do this and you will live." But he, wanting to justify himself, said to Jesus, "And who is my neighbor?" Then Jesus answered and said: "A certain man went down from Jerusalem to Jericho, and fell among thieves, who stripped him of his clothing, wounded him, and departed, leaving him half

dead. Now by chance a certain priest came down that road. And when he saw him, he passed by on the other side. Likewise a Levite, when he arrived at the place, came and looked, and passed by on the other side. But a certain Samaritan, as he journeyed, came where he was. And when he saw him, he had compassion. So he went to him and bandaged his wounds, pouring on oil and wine; and he set him on his own animal, brought him to an inn, and took care of him. On the next day, when he departed, he took out two denarii, gave them to the innkeeper, and said to him, 'Take care of him; and whatever more you spend, when I come again, I will repay you.' So which of these three do you think was neighbor to him who fell among the thieves?" And he said, "He who showed mercy on him." Then Jesus said to him, "Go and do likewise."

While Jesus did not specifically state in His parable the method of transportation for the priest or Levite, by the inclusion of "his own animal" (v. 34), it seems that only the Samaritan had a horse or donkey. Also notice that there is no explanation of why the Levite and the priest passed by— we assume because they were hard-hearted. Perhaps also it was that, lacking an animal, they had no way of helping the man anyway! The Samaritan's response was, "What's mine is yours." He not only tended the man's wounds and put him on his animal, but he paid for the man to recover at an inn. Even then, the Samaritan didn't dump the injured man on the innkeeper. Instead, he said, "Look, if this guy costs you any more money than what I have left, I'll make it up to you when I pass back through."

We don't know if the man was unconscious at that point or not, but if he was awake, the injured man had a golden opportunity to sponge off the innkeeper at the Samaritan's expense, long after he was healed. But the Samaritan did not even worry about that. Let's not forget, though, that not only did the man have the *will* to help the injured man, but he also had the *means*. If that Samaritan had been penniless and didn't have an animal to transport the man, that poor traveler would still have been laying there.

The means to reach a lost world are not cheap. Yes, you can hand out tracts at the beach and maybe reach a few dozen people. However, if you want to make a major impact on the world, consider this: a single broadcast of *Ever Increasing Faith* can reach millions of people by television, but it costs more than thirty thousand dollars an hour to broadcast this program. Printing costs for Bibles and Christian books are no different than printing costs for a best-selling novel. Everything costs money, and money for God's projects has to come from God's people. You and I are in the position of stewards. It's not merely obedience to give 10 percent, but God will ask, "What did you do with that other 90 percent that I entrusted to you?" We will all have to answer to a heavenly audit one day.

BECOMING A COWORKER WITH GOD

In the process of gaining wealth, we become workers together with God in seeking and saving the lost. Many people are not good one-on-one witnesses just because of their personalities. Some are shy and withdrawn, and let's be honest: some people don't have enthralling conversion stories. When the Puritans first came here, they used to require you to be a member of their church before you could vote in city elections. To become a member of the church, you had to sit in front of a group of elders and present your conversion event. To make sure everyone believed you were truly saved you needed to make it a good one! As a result, someone might be tempted to say, "Well, I was drinking a fifth of Jack Daniels a day and living with six women!" Nonetheless, there are those who, like my wife Betty, will tell you that there wasn't a time that she didn't know Jesus, didn't trust her life to Jesus, and so on. She didn't need to be in the gutter, if you will, to know that He was Lord of her life. The point is, while everyone should be a witness, personality differences are such that some people may not be very good at communicating even something as important as their salvation.

The good news is that you don't have to be a public speaker to bring hundreds, even thousands, of people to Jesus. Paul said, "Now you Philippians know also that in the beginning of the gospel, when I departed from Macedonia, no church shared with me concerning giving and receiving but you only. For even in Thessalonica you sent aid once and again for my necessities. Not that I seek the gift, but I seek the fruit that abounds to your account" (Phil. 4:15–17). Whether He was referring to feeding the hungry, or clothing the naked, God established a principle that applies here.

When you have contributed to a ministry that results in the salvation of thousands, it will be counted to you as though you had personally witnessed to each person. You can be a *goer* or you can be a *sender*. Everyone cannot pick up and go to a foreign mission field, but everyone can help send someone who is willing to go.

Once you start to look at it in those terms, wealth becomes a much different quality. It is something to be possessed and used for kingdom purposes. That's why Paul would write to Timothy, "Command those who are rich in this present age"—so there obviously were rich people in the church, and Paul had no problem with them having wealth—"not to be haughty, nor to trust in uncertain riches but in the living God, who gives us richly all things to enjoy" (1 Tim. 6:17). Clearly Paul was saying that if your *trust* is in God, you won't have a problem at all with the riches. What else about those "who are rich in this present age," Paul? "Let them [who are rich in this present age] do good, that they be rich in good works, ready to give, willing to share, storing up for themselves a good foundation for the time to come, that they may lay hold on eternal life" (1 Tim. 6:18–19). Note how that contrasts earlier with the parable Jesus told in Luke 12:13–21 about the man who built new barns, only to find his time was up? Here in 1 Timothy, Paul is saying that you are "storing up...a good foundation" (v. 19).

Again and again we see the order of things: trust in God, then God gives richly. That phrase "who gives us richly all things to enjoy" in 1 Timothy 6:17 literally means "abundantly supplied."[1] Notice Paul did not tell Timothy to have the rich people give away all their money. It has been an erroneous running theme in Christianity for years that if you come to Christ, you have to give up everything and be broke. The devil fed that lie because the last thing he needed was rich, victorious Christians. There are two ways of giving up everything. One is to literally give it all away, but the other—the way the Lord wants you to do it—is to commit it all to the Lord and say, "Lord, what would You have me do with this?" When Paul wrote: "Let them do good, that they be rich in good works, ready to give, willing to share" (1 Tim. 6:18), it reflected God's priority of how Christians should deal with wealth.

Jesus repeatedly fed people—on at least two occasions He fed more than four thousand people at a single setting. Was He in the fast food business? No. He didn't say, "I came to feed." He said, "I came to seek and to save." But before people will listen, their stomachs have to be full. At Crenshaw Christian Center, we have what we call a Community Outreach Program, which costs us more than twenty thousand dollars a week (about one million dollars per year) to provide food and clothing to people in need. Yet we have to use that wisely. Jesus said in Matthew 10:16 that we are to "be wise as serpents and harmless as doves." We are required to prudently use our money to help those in need and to make sure that we give them spiritual food as well.

Even your brain, your talents, and your abilities are not yours. They are the Lord's. Are you an excellent accountant? An exceptional manager? Do you think your local church could use your talents more than that company you work for? Maybe you need to be willing to give and share of your time and talents. How can God trust you with wealth when you won't so much as serve on the church's business committee or assist in the building project to find a bigger building? When we refer to God funneling money to you, it's not a "money in, money out" equation; there's more to it. Now, I'm not talking about your tithe, which is off the table as a topic of discussion. Rather, I'm saying that if God has blessed you richly with talent, but you are selfishly hoarding that talent for your own prosperity, He cannot trust you with more money.

Once again, to be faithful in much, you have to prove yourself faithful in little.

Everyone is gifted in something. While I know people who would go crazy working in the nursery—one woman said she'd "velcro the kids to the wall" after only ten minutes!—there is someplace in the body of Christ where your talents are needed. Are you sharing yourself? This may sound disconnected, but it is not. If you are God's pipeline, you can't be clogged up with any gunk, anywhere.

God wants us to be His co-workers. Paul wrote in 1 Corinthians 3:9, "For we are God's fellow workers; you are God's field, you are God's building." Paul was using a business metaphor. We are God's workshop, His plant floor where things get made. We are laborers with him. Not *for* God, *with Him*. What an honor to be co-workers with the Almighty! That is our calling. Business partners with Him! Well, we can't be effective partners if we aren't doing our part. For us to work with Him, we must tithe and be willing to give.

So, assuming you are tithing and that you are living right, is there anything else you need to do to ensure you receive heavenly blessings? You need to follow your act of confession—the tithe—with a confession of your mouth. Daily, you need to take a stand and say, "I believe I receive my return on my tithe (or offering), and devil, you cannot touch my return. I bind your power in the name of Jesus. I stand on the Word of God, and I believe I receive my return."

In Mark 11:24 Christ instructed, "Therefore I say to you, whatever things you ask when you pray, believe that you receive them, and you will have them." *Them* what? Not "them things" that you asked for—this is where many people get confused. No, what Jesus was saying in Mark is that when you ask, you will only have what you *believe you have received.*

Perhaps you have been tithing and living right, but it hasn't gotten you anything. Are you asking? Maybe you need to adjust your prayer and faith life. Have you worked with some electronic gizmo—say, a DVD projector—and you put in a DVD and…nothing happens. The DVD player is working, you have everything turned on, but the screen is blank. Does that mean the DVD isn't working? No, it's spinning away inside the machine. That signal is coming out, but there is something blocking it. Then all of a sudden you look at the "DVD/VHS" button and realize you have it turned to "VHS." So you push the DVD button, and all of a sudden, the picture is on, the sound is on, and everything is working. Imagine for a second that that DVD was like God in our metaphor: He was doing His part. He kept sending and sending that signal, but you weren't receiving it because you weren't pushing the right button.

James said, "If any of you lacks wisdom, let him ask of God, who gives to all liberally and without reproach, and it will be given to him" (James 1:5). This verse covers all situations where you don't know whether a particular need is "of God." If you don't know, ask. Don't assume because someone is a minister or because someone invokes the name of Jesus that this is a need for which *you* have been called to give.

If you are believing to live debt free, you need to make a daily confession:

> *Father, I thank you for taking care of these debts, however You choose to do it. I thank you for increasing my income or reducing my indebtedness. But however You do it, Father, I receive the answer to my prayer to be debt-free.*

You have to be in a position, financially, that if the Lord says, "Whom shall I send?" you can answer, as did Isaiah, "Here am I! Send me" (Isa. 6:8). But you can't say that if you don't have it. If I say, "We have a pressing need in a particular African country for a hospital and church, and it will cost fifteen million dollars," can you say, "No problem. I'll give a million dollars"? No matter what your heart says, you can't say that if you don't have it. To be a pipeline, something has to be flowing through the pipes!

God wants His children to prosper. Jesus Himself said He came to seek and save those who were lost and that we were to go into all the world and preach the gospel. So the first and most obvious purpose of tithing is that we should all be prosperous, and the reason we should be prosperous is so that we can finance every good work in the kingdom. Job figured this out when he said that God is mighty, and if people "obey and serve Him, They shall spend their days in prosperity, And their years in pleasures" (Job 36:11). John confirmed this when he wrote, "Beloved, I pray that you prosper in all things and be in health, just as your soul prospers" (3 John 2).

Have you ever wondered what would happen if Christians tithed? Sometimes you hear that no one would take care of the poor if the government didn't. Is that true?

The U.S. Census Bureau has a question about religious affiliation, where people mark a box, such as "Christian, Muslim, Buddhist, " and so on. Approximately 87 percent of Americans refer to themselves as Christians on such forms. (Polls actually have this percentage slightly higher.) Other surveys that ask the question, do you attend church regularly? put the number of Christians lower, at around 55 percent. Still other researches found that if they phrase the question, did you attend church last week? the number falls to as low as 20 percent in some polls.[2]

Several years ago, one of the fellows who edits some of my books—a college professor—worked with one of his students to calculate the average income of Christians in America. They did this based on different levels of giving for different denominations in the U.S. Based on population statistics, they then came up with a total dollar figure tithed each year by Christians. It came to about 3 percent of their income. Next, these researchers looked at the amount that would have been generated if all these Christians tithed 10 percent of their incomes. Just for comparison, they looked at what that amount came to, relative to the total budgets for welfare, health, and human services from not only the federal government but all the state and local governments as well. They found that if the most narrowly defined group of Christians—the 27 percent who reported having gone to church the week before actually tithed—the church could provide 125 percent of these governments' welfare, health, and human services budgets. And if all those in America who called themselves Christians actually acted like Christians and tithed, it would produce *225 percent* of all the federal, state, and local welfare/health and human services spending![3]

Christians have more than enough money to meet every need, both in the churches and in their communities. The pipeline could be overflowing. But have you ever, even once, heard anyone in any church say, as the craftsmen said to Moses, "The people bring much more than enough for the service of the work which the LORD commanded us to do" (Ex. 36:5). In other words, they came to Moses and said, "Tell them to stop giving! We can't take any more!" Exodus 36:6 says, "And the people were restrained from bringing." The Bible doesn't tell us specifically, but I think you know the answer: do you think a single one of those people who had to be restrained from giving was lacking for any thing? Wouldn't it be a tremendous legacy for you if it were said after you were gone, "He gave too much," or "She gave beyond measure"? Do you think at that point Jesus would say, "Well done, good and faithful servant?"

Notes

Notes

NOTES

INTRODUCTION

1. Bruce Lindsey, *The Age of Abundance* (New York: HarperCollins, 2007), 281.

2. Ibid.

3. Leroy Thompson, *Money Cometh! To the Body of Christ* (Cincinnati: Harrison House, 1996).

Chapter 1
IS GOD POOR?

1. "List of Billionaires," *Forbes*, March 8, 2007.

2. Discussions and correspondence with Prof. Larry Schweikart, University of Dayton, various dates, 2007.

3. George E. Meisinger, "Judas," *Bible.org*, http://www.bible.org/page.php?page_id=488 (accessed September 24, 2007).

4. Sir William R. Ramsay, *St. Paul, the Traveler and Roman Citizen*, Mark Wilson, ed., (London: Angus Hudson, 2001), 35.

5. Ibid., 235.

6. Ibid., 235.

7. Ibid., 235.

Chapter 3
THE LAW OF TITHES AND OFFERINGS

1. Arthur C. Brookes, *Who Really Cares: America's Charity Divide—Who Gives, Who Doesn't, and Why it Matters* (New York: Basic Books, 2006), 138–139.

Chapter 5
THE WORLD'S PROSPERITY SYSTEM

1. Harold Evans, Gail Buckland, and David Lefer, *They Made America: From the Steam Engine to the Search Engine: Two Centuries of Innovators* (Boston: Back Bay Books, 2006); Forrest McDonald, Insull (Chicago: University of Chicago Press, 1962).

2. For more information see http://www.cfp-board.org/bulletin.html (accessed 9/14/07).

3. Kelly St. John, "Big Lottery Winners Know a Lot About What Not to Do," *San Francisco Chronicle*, February 16, 2002, http://www.geocities.com/ccd4664/BigLottoryWinners.htm (accessed September 24, 2007).

4. Ibid.

5. For more information see http://ucsfhr.ucsf.edu/hrupdate/update200202.htm (accessed 9/14/07).

6. "Money Can't Buy Happiness," *BBCNews.com*, February 12, 2001, http://news.bbc.co.uk/1/hi/health/1162153.stm (accessed September 24, 2007).

7. For more information see https://www.theeap.com/main/content/June%2004%20-%20Study%20Finds%20Satisfaction%20in%20Working.pdf (accessed September 14, 2007).

8. For more information see http://www.gamingmagazine.com/managearticle.asp?c=220&a=1156 (accessed September 14, 2007).

9. Quote from *Rocky III* available at http://www.imdb.com/title/tt0084602/quotes (accessed September 20, 2007).

10. For more information see http://www.vatican.va/holy_father/leo_xiii/encyclicals/documents/hf_l-xiii_enc_15051891_rerum-novarum_en.html (accessed September 14, 2007).

11. Brooks, *Who Really Cares?* 145.

12. Ibid., 150.

13. Ibid.

Chapter 6
The Prosperity Pipeline

1. "The Camel and the Eye of the Needle," *BiblicalHebrew.com,* http://www.biblicalhebrew.com/nt/camelneedle.htm (accessed September 21, 2007).

2. Frederick K. C. Price, *Why Should Christians Suffer?* (Los Angeles: FaithOne, 2005).

3. Chris Gardner, *The Pursuit of Happyness* (New York: Amistad, 2006).

Chapter 7
The Purpose of Prosperity

1. W. E. Vine, *Vine's Expository Dictionary of Old and New Testament Words* (Nashville: Thomas Nelson, 1997, p. 968.

2. C. Kirk Hadaway and P. L. Marler, "Did You Really Go to Church This Week? Behind the Poll Data," *The Christian Century* May 6, 1998, 472-475.

3. Larry Schweikart with Robert Gressis, "Charity Begins at Home: Christianity, Tithing, and the Welfare State," paper presented to the 1996 Economic and Business Historical Society Meeting.

ABOUT THE AUTHOR

D R. FREDERICK K. C. Price is the founder and pastor of Crenshaw Christian Center in Los Angeles, California, and Crenshaw Christian Center East in Manhattan, New York. He is known worldwide as a teacher of the biblical principles of faith, healing, prosperity and the Holy Spirit. During his more than 50 years in ministry, countless lives have been changed by his dynamic and insightful teachings that truly "tell it like it is."

His television program, *Ever Increasing Faith Ministries (EIFM)*, has been broadcast throughout the world for more than 25 years and currently airs in 15 of the 20 largest markets in America, reaching an audience of more than 15 million households each week. *EIFM* is also Webcast on the Internet via www.faithdome.org. The *EIFM* radio program is heard on stations across the world, including the continent of Europe via short-wave radio.

Author of more than 50 popular books teaching practical application of biblical principles, Dr. Price pastors one of America's largest church congregations, with a membership of approximately 22,000. The Los Angeles church sanctuary, the FaithDome, is among the most notable and largest in the nation, with seating capacity of more than 10,000.

In 1990, Dr. Price founded the Fellowship of Inner-City Word of Faith Ministries (FICWFM). Members of FICWFM include more than 300 churches from all over the United States and various countries. The Fellowship, which meets regionally throughout the year and hosts an annual convention, is not a denomination. Its mission is to provide fellowship, leadership, guidance and a spiritual covering for those desiring a standard of excellence in ministry.

Dr. Price holds an honorary doctorate of divinity degree from Oral Roberts University and an honorary diploma from Rhema Bible Training Center.

For more information, to receive a catalog, or to be placed on the EIFM mailing list, please contact:

Crenshaw Christian Center
P.O. Box 90000
Los Angeles CA 90009
(800) 927-3436

Check your local TV or Webcast listing for
Ever Increasing Faith Ministries
or visit our Web site: www.faithdome.org

MORE DYNAMIC TEACHINGS
BY DR. FREDERICK K. C. PRICE

Race, Religion & Racism, Vol. 1:
A Bold Encounter with Division in the Church

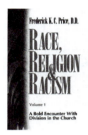

Many of us have turned a blind eye to the most prevalent hate crime in existence today—racism. If we want to please our Heavenly Father the reality of our Christianity has to be manifested in the way we treat one another without prejudice. This teaching that has jolted the church brings light to this satanic evil.

1-883798-36-1: Hardcover
1-883798-81-7: Paperback

Race, Religion & Racism, Vol. 2:
Perverting the Gospel to Subjugate a People

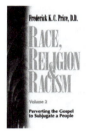

Religion has been the most flagrant perpetrator of racism in the world. And, the church in America has been leading the way. Dr. Price maintains that the church offered support to slave owners and assorted racists by attempting to show that blacks were cursed by God and ranked only slightly above the primates.

1-883798-48-5: Hardcover
1-883798-82-5: Paperback

Race, Religion & Racism, Vol. 3:
Jesus, Christianity & Islam

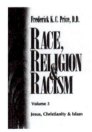

African-Americans have continued to migrate to the teachings of the Nation of Islam. In this, the final volume in the Race, Religion & Racism series, Dr. Price confronts the challenges of Islam based on the Word of God, its ideas, its leaders, and its realities.

1-883798-53-1: Hardcover
1-883798-83-3: Paperback

This teaching is also available on DVD, VHS, CD, and cassette. For the latest information on other books and audio products please contact us at:

(800) 927-3436
Crenshaw Christian Center
P.O. Box 90000
Los Angeles, CA 90009
www.faithdome.org

OTHER RECENT RELEASES
BY DR. FREDERICK K. C. PRICE

Answered Prayer Guaranteed!
The Power of Praying with Faith

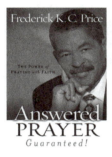

Most Christians struggle with their commitment to prayer and wrestle with a proper prayer attitude and posture. Dr. Price guarantees that if the readers follow his biblically based method, they will have the assurance that God hears their prayers and answers them. He debunks the teaching on prayer that says, "Sometimes God says yes, sometimes He says no, and sometimes He says wait." Too often Christians pray in doubt and unbelief or simply the wrong kind of prayer. Since God responds to faith alone, it is critical for us to understand how to pray in faith and not in doubt, ignorance, or presumption. This book offers a revolutionary approach to prayer!

1-599790-12-2 (Hardcover Book)

How Faith Works:
Special Edition

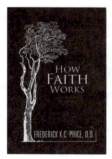

The principles of faith are God's design to bring you everything you will ever need in the earth realm. If you are wondering why some Christians have greater results with the Word of God than others then you need to read this teaching on how to live by faith. Everything in the Kingdom of God is activated by faith, so get this understanding and be empowered.

1-883798-78-7: Leather Bond
1-883798-57-4: Paperback

This teaching is also available on DVD, VHS, CD, and cassette. For the latest information on other books and audio products please contact us at:

(800) 927-3436
Crenshaw Christian Center, P.O. Box 90000
Los Angeles, CA 90009
www.faithdome.org

The Battle of the Mind:
Our Thought Life & Our Armor

You are engaged in a deadly war that takes place in the secrecy of your own mind. Everyone has to fight this battle that goes on in the mind. If you want to be successful in the things of God you will need to control your thought life. When people meditate on what is wrong they become blinded by the problem and never see the escape available to them. Our Heavenly Father has given us a way to bring forth light, and that is through diligent study and meditation of the Word of God. Dr. Price instructs believers on how to control their thought life by utilizing the whole armor of God which is His Word.

CDVD 60 (DVD Set)
CGD 60 (CD Set)

Azusa Convention 2006

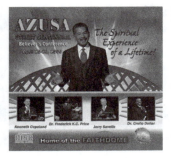

This DVD set archives the Azusa Street Believers' Convention which celebrated the 100-year anniversary of the outpouring of the Holy Spirit in Los Angeles. This spiritual experience of a lifetime is now available on DVD for your visual library. You will hear from the great men of faith, Minister Kenneth Copeland, Minister Jerry Savelle, Dr. Creflo Dollar, and Dr. Price.

AZDV 06 (2-DVD)
AZ06D (4-CD)

These teachings may also be available on VHS and cassette. For the latest information on other books, visual and audio products please contact us at:

(800) 927-3436
www.faithdome.org

F AITH ONE PUBLISHING is the publishing arm of Crenshaw Christian Center in Los Angeles, California, and publisher of *Ever Increasing Faith Magazine.*

Subscribe or Renew your FREE Magazine Subscription

Web site: www.faithdome.org
Call us: (800) 927-3436

This quarterly magazine brings the latest and greatest teachings of Drs. Fred and Betty Price absolutely free to those living in the continental United States. Teachings are geared for the Christian today and cover such areas as:

- Parenting
- Health & Healing
- From the Headlines
- Testimonies
- Missions Work

Keep informed and growing in the things of God by receiving your free copy of this magazine designed to empower you with the Word of Faith.

THE POWER OF FAITH TO TRANSFORM YOUR LIFE!

PROSPERITY

♦

GOOD NEWS FOR GOD'S PEOPLE

FREDERICK K.C. PRICE

FAITH ONE
PUBLISHING

PROSPERITY: GOOD NEWS FOR GOD'S PEOPLE
by Frederick K. C. Price
Published by Faith One Publishing
7901 S. Vermont Avenue
Los Angeles, CA 90044

This book is produced and distributed by Creation House, a part of Strang Communications, www.creationhouse.com.

Unless otherwise noted, all Scripture quotations are from the New King James Version of the Bible. Copyright © 1979, 1980, 1982 by Thomas Nelson, Inc., publishers. Used by permission.

Scripture quotations marked AMP are from the Amplified Bible. Old Testament copyright © 1965, 1987 by the Zondervan Corporation. The Amplified New Testament copyright © 1954, 1958, 1987 by the Lockman Foundation. Used by permission.

Scripture quotations marked NAS are from the New American Standard Bible. Copyright © 1960, 1962, 1963, 1968, 1971, 1972, 1973, 1975, 1977 by the Lockman Foundation. Used by permission. (www.Lockman.org)

Cover design by Justin Evans

Library of Congress Control Number: 2007931866
International Standard Book Number: 978-1-59979-238-5

09 10 11 12 13 — 9 8 7 6 5 4 3
Printed in the United States of America

To
Paul Bergamini S.C.

Fred Price

Mark 11: 24

2010